THE RED McDANIEL STORY will first break your heart; it will then lift your spirits. This is the inspiring, true-life account of one man's courage and perserverance in the face of deprivation and torture in a North Vietnamese prison.

Red McDaniel was shot down over Hanoi during his 81st combat mission in 1967. He was held captive for six years, becoming one of the most brutally tortured prisoners of the Vietnam war.

For his service in Vietnam, Red McDaniel received the Navy's highest award for bravery, The Navy Cross. His many other military decorations include two Silver Stars, two Legions of Merit with combat "V" (for combat valor), two Distinguished Flying Crosses, three Bronze Stars with combat "V", and two Purple Hearts for wounds resulting from the torture he endured as a POW.

After returning home in 1973, Red served as Commanding Officer of USS NIAGARA FALLS and of aircraft carrier USS LEXINGTON. He was Director of Navy/Marine Corps Liaison to the U.S. House of Representatives (1979–1981), after which the Secretary of the Navy personally presented Red with his second Legion of Merit award.

Red continues to work on Capitol Hill as president and founder of the American Defense Foundation (see back page). ADF is active in promoting a strong national defense and in increasing the young American's awareness of and appreciation for America's freedoms.

D0483313

SCARS
AND
STRIPES

*The true story of one man's courage in
facing death as a Vietnam POW.*

by
Captain Eugene B. McDaniel,
USN
with James L. Johnson

The views and opinions expressed in this book are those of the author and do not imply the endorsement of the Department of Defense or other agencies of the United States Government.

The frontispiece drawing is by Lieutenant Commander Mike McGrath, U.S.N.

SCARS AND STRIPES

Formerly published under the name of BEFORE HONOR by A.J. Holman Company, a division of J.B. Lippincott Company, Philadelphia and New York

Library of Congress Catalog Card Number: 79-56818
ISBN 0-89081-231-4

Reprinted by permission of A.J. Holman Company, Broadman Press, Harvest House Publishers, James L. Johnson

Printed in the United States of America

SCARS
AND
STRIPES

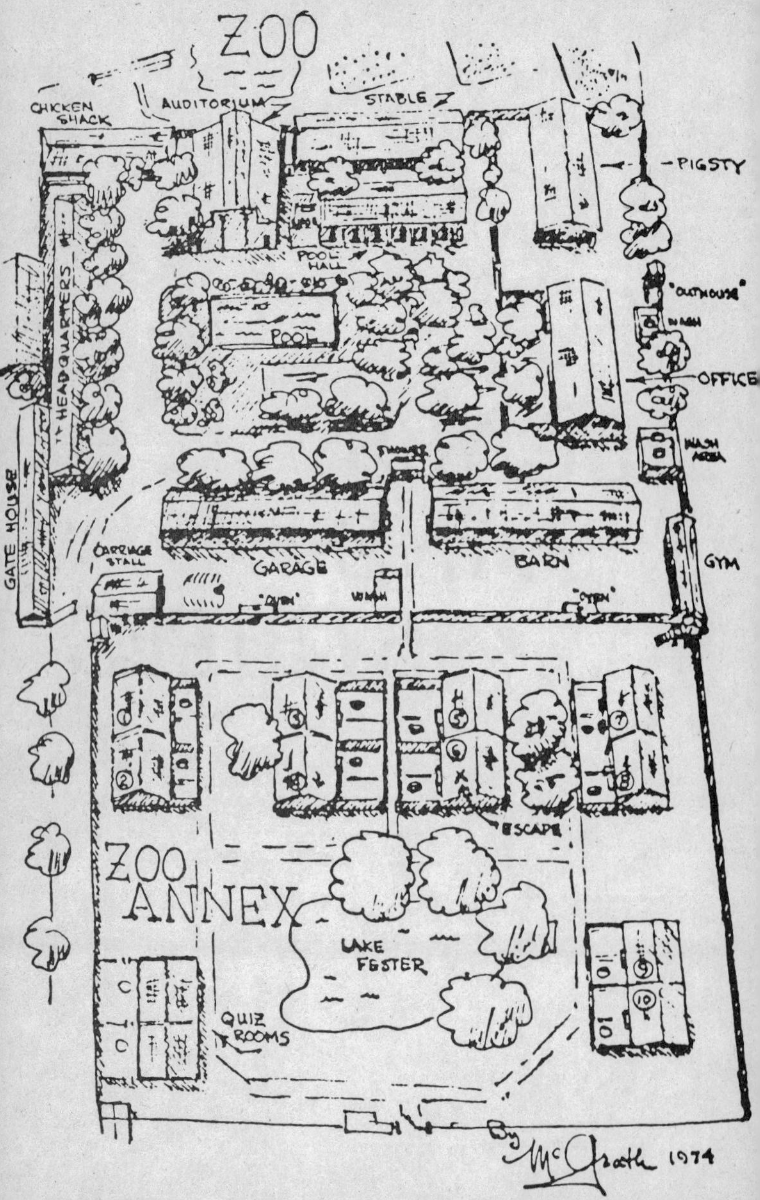

ZOO

CHICKEN SHACK AUDITORIUM STABLE — PIGSTY

POOL HALL "OUTHOUSE" WASH

HEADQUARTERS POOL OFFICE

WASH AREA

GATE HOUSE

CARRIAGE STALL GARAGE "MEN" "WOMAN" BARN "MEN" GYM

ZOO ANNEX

① ② ③ ④ ⑤ ⑥ ⑦ ⑧

ESCAPE

LAKE FESTER

QUIZ ROOMS

⑨ ⑩

By McGrath 1974

To my Bombardier-Navigator,
Lieutenant James Kelly Patterson,
and others like him who did not return

THE McDANIEL FAMILY, 1981

Contents

An eight-page section of photographs follows p. 192

Please help Red McDaniel keep America strong through the 'American Defense Foundation. See inside back cover.

". . . before honor is humility."

Proverbs 18:12

1

The Alpha Flight: Van Dien

I AWOKE TO THE SHORT, raucous jangle of the phone on the wall over my head, giving me a rude jab as if to say I ought to be ashamed that I was caught sleeping.

I fumbled for it in the semidarkness of my quarters, picked it up. On the other end was the voice of the duty officer, Rod Bankson.

"You have a brief in a half hour," he said shortly. Concise, to the point, as all duty officers had to be.

I cleared my throat, conscious of the light roll of the carrier *Enterprise* under me, gently tipping me right and left as if I were in a bassinet getting the rock-a-bye treatment.

"What's the target?" I asked, and the sound of my voice was carrying maybe just a trace of apprehension above the hoarseness of sleep.

"It's an Alpha Strike," Bankson replied in a straight, unemotional tone, as if "Alpha Strike" were nothing more than delivering mail to a company of Waves at Waikiki. Actually, an Alpha Strike meant a maximum effort into North Vietnam planned by the Joint Chiefs of Staff in Washington.

"Where?" I asked Bankson, hoping it might be a well-plowed target with not too much flak concentration.

"Van Dien."

I didn't say anything to Bankson for a long ten seconds,

it seemed; I hung onto the receiver, wanting to argue, feeling the familiar rumble of *Enterprise*'s power plant around me. I had already flown eighty missions over Vietnam, fifteen of them Alpha Strikes. Only two days ago, May 17, I had gone on an Alpha Strike to Package 6 to knock out a bridge south of Hanoi. It was VFR (Visual Flight Rules) all the way, which meant the VC ground gunners had us zeroed in on the entire run over the target. It was tough. When I got back after that, I figured I had a breather coming. Instead, I now had Van Dien on the menu—a truck repair center just south of Hanoi, a place we called "Little Detroit"—and the odds were the VC would be throwing everything they had at us.

Yet, as I sought for something to say to Bankson, I was caught in the dilemma that every naval pilot faces: I had to keep going up on the Alpha Strikes as well as the milk runs if I intended to get my command. And, what's more, if I could get in ninety-one or ninety-two missions, I would be rotated out of the combat zone.

So I said, "Okay," and hung up the phone. It was a little after six in the morning; I got up and went through the motions of preparation for the Alpha missions inside North Vietnam. I shaved first, but did not use after-shave lotion or deodorant. In case I were shot down, as the regulations had it, the VC, who did not use body lotion or deodorant, could smell it for hundreds of yards and zero in on me. But, even as I finished shaving, I did not consider being shot down and taken prisoner. The chances of being killed were more real, and for this I had to prepare my mind every morning. For one thing, getting hit in an A-6 jet, carrying all those thousand-pounders under the wings, did not offer too much time to blow canopy and parachute down. And it was the bombing approach where the flak was heaviest and the chances of getting hit were the highest. If I *was* hit, chances were that I would either blow up with the aircraft or ride her down, unable to get out. Death, then, was the real risk of the maximum efforts into North Vietnam, not the possibility of living or being captured, though there were those who had lived and been captured.

So now, having finished the shave, I ran my fingers over the smooth skin of my face and took a few minutes to reflect. I was thirty-five years old, still showing the reddish-blond hair that had pegged me "Red" since the year one. The blue eyes were clear enough yet, though there were little crinkles beginning to show underneath which said I was a veteran military man in more ways than one. I was still in good shape physically, keeping my weight evenly distributed across my six-foot three-inch frame through disciplined exercise, a habit I had carried over from my athletic days in high school and college. My twelve years in naval aviation had also drilled into me the need to stay on the line mentally and physically, so I really didn't have to back off to the younger men in the squadron—at least not yet.

For some reason on this day, however, I kept feeling a nagging kind of doubt. I was the father of three children back in Virginia Beach, Virginia. I had a beautiful wife, Dorothy, whom I had courted in college and who was everything I needed to complement my life. But today I felt some grittiness—maybe uncertainty?—about the mission coming up. Like all combat men, I supposed, after so many maximum missions, exhaustion begins to dig in. Or maybe right then I missed Dorothy more acutely; I felt the need to be home with her and the kids like other fathers who had banking or real estate jobs. But here I was, preparing for my eighty-first mission countdown, ten thousand miles from home, the nibbling fear that maybe death was waiting for me today, that I would not see my family again . . . and somehow I wanted my death to be worthy of them.

I felt disturbed by these feelings, because I never allowed myself to think along such lines. I was, after all, a military man; I had chosen it for my career. In choosing it, I lived by the demands of it—it was a fraternity of men who stuck by the spirit and the rule, Ours not to reason why, ours but to do and (sometimes) die. We believed in our commanders, in our President, and in the cause, no matter how marginal or confusing at times, and every military man since the beginning stuck by that and delivered the goods as best he could. I believed that what we were doing in Vietnam was right, that we were trying to contain Communist aggression. And even if the South Vietnamese didn't particularly care whether democracy or a dictatorship ruled their lives, the point was that the United States was trying to draw the line here for the Free World. Only history could determine whether it was right or wrong.

I had come to that conviction a long time ago or else I wouldn't have eighty combat missions behind me. So why was I feeling doubts about it today? I had been chafing for a couple of days now; maybe it was a kind of growing resentment at having to take so many missions deep into North Vietnam. The more experience I got flying those Alpha Strikes, the more missions I was asked to take, and, though I knew that was the natural order of things in the military combat strategy, each new deep penetration into North Vietnam increased my chances of getting shot down. Each mission lately was marked by heavier and more accurate antiaircraft fire, including the dreaded SAMs (surface-to-air missiles). I still remembered the Alpha mission over Nam Dinh back in February, one of the toughest targets south of Hanoi. The North Vietnamese told a *New York Times* correspondent that Nam Dinh was a "peaceful textile center," but going over it on a bombing run proved other than peaceful. As Lieutenant James Kelly Patterson, my bombardier-navigator, said of it that night, "The North Vietnamese threw up more steel than we dropped." And, after landing safely on *Enterprise* that night, I smoked a cigarette, the first I had had in two years—a sure sign the tension had gotten to me. Now to have to go deeper and closer to Hanoi, to Van Dien, a critical vehicle repair center, meant a certain tougher show all the way around. Thinking about it, I began to tense up like all pilots did. Kelly Patterson once described what it's like the night before the mission: "You can't sleep, you can't eat, your bladder's always full, your mouth is dry."

Then he added what I was like as we went in on the target, "McDaniel pants like a puppy dog every time we get near the place." He was right—and already I was beginning to get those sensations in anticipation.

But there was something else, too. I did not relish particularly having to blast the target we had for these missions. I knew that, as careful as we were about where we put our bombs, some probably did kill and hurt civilians. I knew that it was as tough on the people on the ground as it was on us making those runs over the target. As much as I knew how necessary it was to cripple the North Vietnamese war effort to the point that a decent peace settlement could be negotiated, the price being paid was steep on both sides. Putting that together with the growing unpopularity of the war at home, the uncertainty as to whether all the punishment we were inflicting on the North Vietnamese was accomplishing what was intended, right then I wanted the war to end as I never had—for the sake of the Vietnamese as well as ourselves. It wasn't going to end today, however, nor would there be a reprieve. I had been hoping, like everybody else on *Enterprise*, that we would be rotated out of the line—we were past due—to head for the Philippines for some much-needed liberty. But now I could hear the sounds of *Enterprise*'s machinery gearing up for the launch, and there just wasn't time to mull over these doubts anymore.

So I finished dressing, still feeling mildly gritty, and went up to breakfast. Normally I would go to the Ready Room first, but today there was time to spare. Oddly enough, I ate well—bacon and eggs and all the trimmings, then went back for a Western omelet. I ate only half of it, though, and left the rest. I was to remember that half-eaten omelet a long time in the months and years ahead.

With breakfast finished, I went up to the IOIC (Integrated Operations Intelligence Center) for the first briefing with the air wing, which would comprise about twenty-six aircraft. Here with the wing, I got the weather and studied the photographs of the target and the rendezvous point. Finished, I moved down to the Squadron Ready Room, where those in my immediate squadron compared notes on the course and the safety procedures to follow within the wing. I would be flying Number 3, behind our leader, Commander Herm Turk.

Then we were moving up to the deck and the A-6 Intruder, and as I went out to the plane, Commander Michaels, who was the chaplain, lifted his thumb to me. We had talked a lot together in the months past, because he was from North Carolina, my home territory, and because he "had the faith" as I did. Now he was trying to tell me it was going to be okay. It was good to have that gesture, because Michaels knew we were in an Alpha Strike too. As I preflighted the aircraft along with Kelly Patterson, Captain J. L. Holloway III,* skipper of the ship, tapped me on the leg and said, "A good day, Red! No sweat! You'll be going in behind the Air Force and there will be two big raids before you get there. By the time you get over the target, there'll be no flak to worry about. You'll have a good mission!"

Two good omens? I didn't know. There wasn't much time to analyze these things. I climbed up the boarding ladder and slipped into the cockpit. Kelly Patterson strapped in next to me. We were side by side, in this ungainly twin-jet bomber that looks like a clumsy beetle at best, separated by a line of switches and knobs on a floor console between our seats. The A-6 had been the workhorse for the Navy since 1962 and, despite her awkward looks, could strike targets regardless of weather or the time of day. She was a flying computer, using what is called the DIANE (Digital Integrated Attack Navigational Equipment) system. Kelly's job was to program the course to the target and all the information related to the mission on a typewriter keyboard in front of him. The computer took us the rest of the way. The only thing Kelly could not do was program in our life chances in that mission; that was still in the hands of God.

I ran up the two J-52 jet engines, taxied down to the catapult, and locked into it. As we sat there, we ran down the familiar cockpit check.

* Presently Chief of Naval Operations.

"Wings." Kelly snapped it off at me.

"Wings spread and locked . . . handle stowed, flags flush . . ."

"Flaps?"

"Flaps in takeoff . . . slats down . . . stabilizer shifted . . . speed brakes in . . ."

"Trim . . . checked?"

"Checked. Zero rudder, zero aileron . . . six units nose up . . ."

"Fuel?"

"Fuel checked . . . five switches up . . . pressurization switches normal . . . wing-pressure lights out . . . fuel ready switch off . . . fuel gauge shows fifteen thousand pounds . . ."

"Controls?"

"Controls free . . ."

"Seats?"

"Seats armed top and bottom . . . harness locked . . . check yours . . ."

"Set, ready to go . . ."

"Roger."

The sound of Kelly's voice was always pleasant and reassuring to me. We had flown together for eighteen months, almost seven hundred flight hours together. I knew his every move; he knew mine. He was twenty-six years old, round-faced, pleasant. And sensitive. Kelly would never let his bombs go if the target was at all in question due to a weak radar signal. For him, life was too precious just to let fly with destruction at anything in North Vietnam. I admired him for that virtue, among many others, and this made our comradeship something deep and vital.

Kelly had a brother in Vietnam fighting with the infantry in the South. Whenever Kelly got leave he would find his brother and go on patrol with him just so he could be with him. To me, that was the kind of love that didn't come down the street every day.

Now I ran over the rows of gauges in front of me, my eyes flicking over them almost automatically, knowing what to look for after so many flights, waiting for the catapult shot that would put us at flying speed off the carrier in two seconds. As I glanced out to focus on the catapult officer below, waving his hand over his head to build us up for the final go, I thought of the 13,000 pounds of bombs under my wings again, the 15,000 pounds of fuel, the 28,000 pounds that went with the aircraft proper. Something like 58,000 pounds had to get airborne off that catapult, and as many times as I went through this final second before the shot, I never got totally comfortable about the thought of landing in the drink with all that weight.

Then the catapult officer's hand was at the peak of his windup. I gave him the salute, and I felt the shock of the catapult against the back of my head where it rested firmly up against the headrest. I had control of the aircraft in those two seconds, and began the climb out to rendezvous with the squadron.

I didn't look back or down. I kept my eyes out for my grouping flight. I knew, though, the friendly deck of *Enterprise* was getting smaller all the time as we climbed. I was glad I didn't look back . . . somehow today I wanted to get the mission over with as fast as I could . . . I wanted to look at *Enterprise* on the return approach, not outward bound. And maybe that, too, was a kind of omen. . . .

We rendezvoused at fifteen thousand feet off the coast of North Vietnam. For some reason I had trouble getting into position in the flight, and it bothered me. I didn't seem to be with it today, but after a while we got ourselves straightened out and joined up with the wing. We moved on over North Vietnam, and I felt a great sense of camaraderie with all those aircraft around, flying so close together in a perfect formation. Being so near to one another and aware of all that power there is under you, you get a feeling that erases whatever fear you have.

I remember going over the beach at Thanh Hoa, where we called "Feet Dry," meaning we were over dry land now. The first thirty to forty miles inland were uneventful—a little small-arms flak, but we had the cover of the clouds to help us. At about sixty miles we started seeing the SAM missiles coming up. They are like telephone poles with fins on one end. We could look ahead and see a SAM exploding.

We turned to a compass heading of 034, which was the final attack heading, and fixed on Van Dien, just south of the city of Hanoi. Now we began maneuvering more—"jinking," as we called it—to avoid those SAMs coming up around us. My fingers were tense on the control stick as I maneuvered right and left, and it was easy to understand why I was a member of the "white-knuckle club" with other pilots who had come through this pattern. With twenty-six aircraft around us, all jinking, I had to sweat over not only the SAMs, but also the possibility of collision with a wingman.

Suddenly I got a red light on my ECM (electronic countermeasure). Along with it came a warbling sound in my headset, like a French ambulance hooting—which meant that radar on the ground had locked on to me and was tracking and a SAM would be coming up on us soon.

"Ray Gun Lead, Ray Gun Three," I said over the radio to lead pilot Herm Turk. "I have a blinking red."

He acknowledged, but apparently no one else in the flight was locked on from the ground. I kept on jinking to avoid the three other SAMs that had come up aimed at our squadron. After twenty to twenty-five seconds of dodging, Turk came on and said, "Ray Gun Three, do you still have a blinking red?"

"Affirmative."

At the same moment, Nick Carpenter, flying Turk's other wing, said over the radio, "Missile, ten o'clock!"

I was still trying to avoid the No. 4 SAM then, and before I could concentrate on that new one somewhere off to the left, I heard a violent blast, jarring our aircraft with a turbulent shock, forcing me to fight the controls to hold the plane. I knew I must have been hit by that No. 5 SAM, which I never did see. At the same instant, my wingman—Ray Gun Four, Steve Owen—shouted, "I'm hit!" I sensed what had happened then: the fifth SAM, the one I had not seen, had gone off between our planes, and we had both taken the shrapnel it sprayed on explosion. The SAM is designed to go off after coming within a certain distance of metal—in this case, the metal of our aircraft. Now I felt the nose of my plane pitch down, and the red lights on the console in front of me began stabbing out the message that we had a fire in our port engine. Meanwhile my VDI (Visual Display Indicator), a nine-inch TV screen showing my flight path in relation to ground, indicated I was sliding off and down to the right. We had lost all our hydraulic systems, so I had no control, and we were going in at a twenty-degree down angle, picking up speed as we went. There is no feeling quite like knowing there was nothing I could do to change what was happening. I kept trying to pull the control stick, but it was frozen solid.

Quickly I got on the radio and said, "We've lost both hydraulic systems. We're heading for the hills." In reality, however, we were heading wherever the plane took us, but I could see the mountain ranges ahead of us and felt that we might just get that far anyway.

"Let's get out!" Kelly yelled at me.

I looked down. It was a clear, flat area, and if we ejected it was a sure thing we'd be captured within five minutes after touching the ground. So I pointed out the hills ahead of us to Kelly; we held a conference—a very brief one—on what to do and opted to try for them. This meant we had to ride our burning aircraft all the way, and, with fuel and rockets under our wings, the chances were lessening with every passing second that we could avoid being blown up. I also noticed that we were riding down even faster—we were near the speed of sound, at 550 knots—and we were not supposed to eject at over 500 knots. At that speed the canopy could jam. But there was hardly time to make choices—anyway, we really had none now.

At two thousand feet just above a three-thousand-foot mountain range, Kelly ejected. I felt all the debris in the bottom of the cockpit come rushing up when he blew out. Then I was blown free, and I felt an intense pain in my left knee as I shot out of the cockpit. There was that one second of being propelled into space, a sickening kind of floating somersault that doesn't seem to end; then came a jarring jerk that rattled my entire body, and I knew the chute had opened over me.

I could look down now and see the ground beginning to come up. Kelly's chute was still visible going in far off to the right on the other side of the mountain range. I watched our crippled A-6 go down and smash into the mountain with a puff of yellow flame followed by a pillar of black smoke. My parachute was oscillating far too much on the descent, swinging me to the right and left; I tried to control it with the guidelines but with little success. All the time I worked at it I was conscious too that the Vietnamese were firing at me from the ground, because I was still fair game to them until I hit the trees below. Finally, unable to get the chute controlled, I glanced up to see if I could spot the trouble and noticed a few jagged holes in the silk which apparently had been the result of that high-speed ejection. That explained why I was descending so fast—and that, along with this oscillating effect, meant I could not control where I wanted to land. Worse yet, I was sure I could not survive the impact at the speed I was going. All I could do then was simply hang onto the shroud lines and watch the jungle come rushing up at me until the palm leaves were so large I could see the veins in them.

The minute I hit the tree I crossed my legs as I was instructed to do to keep limbs from hitting my crotch, and then reached out to try to break my slamming descent through the branches. But I went on down, like a block of cement in an elevator shaft. Then I felt a sudden jerk. I was hung up, dangling a good thirty to forty feet off the ground, the easiest target in the world. For a moment it was almost peaceful, after that wild ride down, and I took a while to look around as I swayed gently in the harness. I could see a few hamlets in the distance. Undoubtedly, Vietnamese farmers had seen me come down from where they were, so I had to work fast and get to the ground quickly if I were to avoid them. But now I realized that, once I cut myself free, I had yet another problem: How was I going to survive that forty-foot drop to the ground without serious injury?

I had never expected to be shot down or parachute into the jungle, so now every move was going to be new to me, every step uncertain. I was down, I was alive, but I was still fair game for what I had not anticipated at all—the pursuit of the enemy on the ground.

2

The Jungle

THERE IS NO FEELING quite like knowing you are in a strange country, surrounded by a people who know no rule but death to the enemy. On top of that, of course, is the jungle. There is nothing compared to tropical jungle when it comes to survival. It is thick, thorny, full of unexpected dangers, ruthlessly hot and defiant of man. Flying over it is bad enough—even then it appears sullen, unyielding, merciless—but on the ground a man is soon aware of its immensity, its gigantic suffocating encirclement, its relentless squeeze on life systems that depend on air, good water, and food.

Hanging in my chute harness that forty feet off the ground, I figured I had to take my chances in the jungle rather than become a prisoner. Instead of cutting myself loose, therefore, I crawled up the risers of my chute, hoping to get up to a big limb and climb down the tree to the ground. I managed to climb up about two-thirds of the way and was about six feet from the big branch when it split loose from the tree trunk. I dropped more than forty feet and hit the ground at a sixty-degree incline in a kind of glancing blow. I lay there stunned, feeling the painful muscle spasms in my back. I didn't think I was badly hurt, but unknown to me then I had crushed two vertebrae. After maybe ten minutes I started moving, knowing I had to become mobile or I would be found there. Even as I sat up slowly, I saw the aircraft circle overhead. This was my backup cover man, checking me out to see if I had gone in okay. I searched around my flight suit, found the survival radio, and made contact. I told them I had an injured back but was okay—which meant to them I was not dying at least. They "rogered" and I got up slowly and started moving around in the jungle, half crawling as I went.

I took my G suit off, buried it with the parachute, and strapped on my survival kit. I was dripping wet with sweat by then. It was a little past noon, the sun high up and murderous. But I worked at crawling up that long incline most of the afternoon, now and then stopping to listen to the whistles blowing in the jungle, meaning the Vietnamese were trying to find me. I kept my goal in sight: to get to the top of this incline, which was about a thousand feet away through a jungle as thick as a giant hedge. If I could get to the top, I might be able to contact Kelly, who had gone down on the other side. We had agreed that if we ever ended up in the jungle separated, we would stay in contact with each other by radio. I kept trying to raise him that way all afternoon, but I got nothing.

Sometime later in the afternoon, sweat-soaked, totally exhausted, the jungle beginning its relentless squeeze on my resolve, I heard what I thought were footsteps. On impulse, anxious for contact with Kelly, I yelled his name, figuring he might be stumbling around out there looking for me. With only an hour and a half or so of light left, any VC search party surely would have retreated down the mountain, concluding they couldn't do much up here in the dark. But there was no answering call from the curtains of silent mossy green around me, and I concealed myself again and tried moving further up that mountain.

Finally it was dark, and I had to stop. I took out my survival kit, applied mosquito repellent, and put the mosquito net over my head and my hands. It helped, even though all the insect bites I had gotten from the time I had landed in that tree continued to sting and itch. Straddling a tree trunk about a foot in diameter, I managed to fall asleep on this steep slope.

Some time during the night I awoke to a peculiar roaring sound in the jungle around me, growing in intensity. Then it began to rain, and I realized the sound was that of the rain hitting the trees. I got out my tarpaulin and spread it out to collect the water. I needed water badly. I had drunk all the water I had when I landed earlier, thinking I would be rescued before I needed any more. Now I realized that was a foolish move. I had been without water now for ten hours, and my attempts to trap that rainwater on the tarpaulin were not very successful. I got a little in my mouth from the downpour, but it was at best a torturing teaser.

About ten o'clock that night a propeller aircraft flew overhead with its lights on, and I figured this had to be one of ours trying to spot me, so I got on the radio and simply said, "This is a downed American airman." I got no response. For all I knew, maybe it wasn't one of ours.

So I lay there in that peculiar, uncomfortable position, feeling the press of the dark, brooding jungle around me, thinking of my wife and family. I wondered what Dorothy would think when she was told. My last letter to her had mentioned only that I would be in port, and the one I had sent about moving out on extended line duty would not have arrived yet. She would be relaxed about me, so when the news came about my being shot down it would hit harder.

Then I felt a sudden elation about the fact that I was wounded, because that meant no combat flying for a while. When I got back, which surely would be at daylight, I would have a few months maybe in which to recuperate. The thought of being relieved of having to fly those missions over Vietnam seemed to make my present circumstances less significant. I had not realized up until then the strain of facing the line every day, the flak, the SAM missiles, the "white-knuckle" alley. The very thought of reprieve from it all, the new sense of optimism that came over me just thinking about it, made me realize how much tension I'd been carrying for so long.

So it was going to be sweet flying out of this place in the morning—and I prayed for it. I prayed for rescue as I had never prayed for anything before. When I stopped to think about it, I couldn't remember when I had to pray for anything really crucial like this. I had been a Christian since my freshman year in college. I was a deacon in a Southern Baptist church. I had a faith that I believed was adequate for myself. But I had never been pushed very far to test it for anything—until now. My life had always run on a well-plotted course. God was good for character and meaning in life, for values and stability.

But when had God or Christ become crucial for me?

I remembered the prayer around the dinner table in that simple sharecropper's home where I grew up, the eldest of eight children. It was a familiar prayer, maybe said in haste, but it was meaningful—there was love in it. My parents, being so poor, didn't go to church often because they didn't have the clothes. Now and then they made it, but the experience meant little to me, even though that mealtime prayer did.

Sometimes I went to church with my friends, but it was strictly in order to use the gym. Once in a while I'd go to get in on the social bit, but that, too, meant nothing to me.

Athletics was really my bag. Everything else took second place, including God and church. In high school I was beginning to shape up into a good basketball player, but baseball was more natural to me. If I kept at it, I knew I was going to make it. In fact, I was offered a good chunk of money to play professional when I was in high school. It was more money than my father had made in a lifetime. My father, however—as avid an athletics fan as he was—advised me to go on with college instead; having only finished the fourth grade himself, he knew the value of an education.

I received an athletic scholarship later to Campbell Junior College, a Baptist school in Buies Creek, North Carolina. On registering the first day, I came to the question: "Are you a Christian?" I didn't know how to answer that. I believed in God and Christ, but I wasn't sure what I had that would qualify me for the title "Christian." But I put "Yes" down anyway; after all, I was at Campbell for athletics, not religion, so it really didn't count in the end. But I knew, deep down, that it did.

That same night, I met Dorothy Howard. I had met her earlier in the summer and was impressed. She had dark hair and big blue eyes and a grace and poise about her that made me want to be around her. I knew she was registering at Campbell too, so that night I went to church looking for her and found her. I asked her if I could walk her home, and she agreed. I kept dating her after that, but she always kept me at a safe distance. There were many things that impressed me about her, but sorting them all out I figured it wasn't only her beauty and charm and poise but her character and her sense of values, which were deeply rooted in her belief in God. Her father was a Baptist minister and taught Bible at Campbell, and I got to know him quite well when we drove him to his meetings now and then. His simple faith and absolute sureness about Christ burrowed down into me, and I came to realize more and more that what he and Dorothy had in God was as solid as gold.

I remembered the night an evangelist came to Buies Creek when I was still in my freshman year. I don't remember all he said—in fact, not much of it. But there was something about him—like Dorothy's father—that was right. It was not in all that he said, but in what he appeared to be; his life was 100 percent behind the words. What Dorothy and her father had given me in the months I had been around them, what I knew inwardly was right about God and Christ, came to a head in that meeting. I knew then that it wasn't enough just to believe that God was there or that Christ was a true figure in history but that He had come to give of Himself to a person. I sensed the rightness and truthfulness of the preacher's statement too—that in order to know Christ, what He came to give in salvation, a person had to make that decisive act of receiving who He is and committing all to Him. I didn't understand all the theology of it or how it all worked out finally, but when that preacher asked for "commitment" that night, I simply walked forward to the altar to indicate my willingness to do just that.

I don't remember any big splash with that decision to let Christ have my life. Maybe there should have been more; maybe I should have followed it up with some attempt to find out what really had happened in that "transaction with Christ." I knew something had happened in me as a result of that experience, but I wasn't sure how to translate it into everyday life or whether I really should try.

At any rate, I went on to finish at Campbell and decided to pursue my studies at Elon College. In my junior year my father died, and I was jolted into the realization of what he had left me—that education was not something second best. Up to that time I had gone through college almost untouched by education. So I buckled down and started whipping my courses. Six years after I met Dorothy on campus, we were married. I had enlisted in the Navy for aviation, but I don't know why I picked flying above anything else, except that it seemed to complement my athletic desires. After four months of training in Corpus Christi, Dorothy and I moved to Virginia Beach; there I was baptized into the church and made a deacon. It seemed that this was what Christ had in mind then in my commitment to Him, and I was content to accept that as the totality of His desire and will for me.

But what did that all mean right now as I slapped at mosquitoes and tried to ignore the pain in my knee and my back, trying to get some sleep in the blackness of the jungle around me? I figured I had been pretty straight with the Lord in the past years; I had kept my vows. I had tried to be as straight in my faith as I was on the playing field with the rules of the game. I didn't argue with God about His decisions in life, even when He called me "out" on some pretty close ones. I tried to live up to what I thought He expected of me—being a good husband and father and trying to attain the kind of character He would expect, even in the military, where it wasn't always readily accepted.

So now, hanging onto the one hope I had of rescue, conscious of the sounds around me in the jungle, the cracking branches and the chatter of monkeys, I kept turning the phrase over and over, "Why me? God, why me?" Maybe it was a silly question, but somehow I figured that having Christ in my life, allowing Him to control it—though I was never sure what that meant—sort of gave me a little more power to negotiate the tough spots in life than those who did not have Him. And, as the loneliness and hostility of the jungle pressed down harder on me, I figured maybe Christ owed me something right now—like one of the nice, big, Jolly Green Giant USAF rescue helicopters, which were based in Thailand, hanging over me come dawn.

So my prayers stayed on that subject most of the night, moving from what Christ owed me now in terms of that helicopter rescue to an even more positive level, which was a little like trying to move God closer toward me: "God, thank You for the rescue coming in the morning."

Then after a while I began to feel sluggish and sleepy, and as I dozed off I could still hear those funny sounds around me, the cracking of the twigs, and something kept telling me that those sounds couldn't all be due to monkeys. But my will to stay awake and be sure wouldn't hold, and I slipped off into a cottony kind of doze, the sounds fading off the wide screen of my mind.

I was up at the crack of dawn, around 5:30, feeling the pain and stiffness more than ever, my senses alert, the tingle of excitement and wariness hitting me all at once. I climbed off that tree trunk where I had dozed fitfully in the dark hours and made my way back down the hill I had come up. I thought of Kelly again, wondering where he was and why he hadn't contacted me. As I moved down that hill, I kept pulling off leeches that had grabbed onto my skin. Always there were those sounds of twigs snapping, and I tried to see where those monkeys might be frolicking, just to be sure. But I couldn't see anything in the tangle of trees around me.

It was a good three hundred yards back down the hill to where I had buried my parachute. When I got there I dug it up and made ready to spread it out for the planes that would be coming over me. At 6 A.M. I saw an American A-6 coming my way, accompanied by an F-4 fighter. My hopes leaped afresh. I got out my radio and contacted them, while pulling my parachute open and spreading it out for them to see. Then I heard the pilot say, "I'm over you now," and I recognized the voice of Lieutenant Nicholas Carpenter, and it was the greatest moment for me to hear one of my own.

"Are the Jolly Greens coming, Nick?" I said into the radio.

"Wait one," Nick said, and there was a pause during which I knew he would be checking out that information on the Jolly Greens. In five minutes he came on and said, "They'll be here in forty-five minutes."

"Outstanding," I shouted back.

"See you back on the ship," Nick said, and the plane made one more pass over, rocking its wings, and then was gone.

It was five minutes after six. By 6:45 I would be out and on my way back. So I put all my eggs into one basket—which was to be my undoing. I should have figured that, being on the hill like that, the VC could spot that parachute of mine too. But I figured it would take them time to get to me even if they did locate me, and that the Jolly Greens surely would get to me first. I kept checking the time: 6:30; then 6:45; then up to 7:00. Still no sign of the copters. I began to sweat in the sun again, but a lot of it was from growing concern that I wasn't going to get the pickup. I couldn't understand why. The Air Force was usually on time with their helicopters for rescues of downed air personnel. It was not more than one hundred miles from my present position to their base in Laos. They could come zooming in here down close to the deck so that Vietnamese radar could not pick them up on their screens, and there was therefore no flak to worry about.

When ten o'clock came and passed, then eleven, I knew I was in for it. I debated whether to move out, because the longer I stayed in that spot the greater were the chances of the VC finding me. Yet I had to hope that the helicopters had only been delayed, had the position wrong; and the thing to do in that case was to stay where Nick Carpenter had told them I was.

It was going on one o'clock in the afternoon when I heard the shot. It was close, too close. I turned around and looked up. They were there. Just two Vietnamese about twenty-five feet away. I had my pistol in my hand and made a move to throw it away, and this frightened them. They shot again over my head. I threw the gun down and raised my hands over my head. In a minute or so fifteen Vietnamese civilians were around me. They had a mangy dog with them. They were all barefooted, except for a couple who wore sandals made out of a rubber tire. I noticed their feet were bleeding, which meant they had been moving around all night looking for me; that explained the sounds I had heard in the night and this morning.

So now I simply stood there staring back at them, conscious of how little they seemed in their floppy, pajamalike clothes, not sure of themselves even now that they had me. This was "the enemy," I thought, but looking at them, all I could think of was that they appeared to be more like a bunch of kids out in the jungle looking for something to do.

I was soon to find out differently; I was about to be introduced to a people fanatically dedicated in the military and political senses.

All I could feel then was dejection and that big question: "Where is the Air Force?" And another big one: "God, where are You?"

3

The Grim Reality

ALL THE INFORMATION I had about the nature of the Oriental attitude toward Americans in war right then did not seem to matter much. I had read and studied some about Americans in Japanese prison camps. I had been given some instructions as to what to expect from the North Vietnamese. As these short, jabbering farmers tied my hands behind my back, however, I did not feel any fear they would or even could deal me any great harm. They seemed as much awestruck by my size and what and whom I represented as I was of their smallness.

But when I tried to get their sympathy for my badly swollen knee and my back they showed no response at all. Instead they prodded me up and forced me to start walking, which was really painful. One of them moved out in front and began cutting a path through the jungle with his bolo knife; the rest stayed close in around me. After an hour and a half or so, we arrived at a small hamlet, one of those I had spotted when I was hanging in my chute in that tree. They put me in a small room and stripped me of everything I had, except my undershorts. I was still tied, my hands and arms now swollen and numb from the tightness of the ropes. They loosened them long enough to let me eat some pork fat and greens, but I was not hungry. I was maddeningly thirsty, however, but my attempts to convey that to them got nowhere.

After an hour or so they gave me my flight suit and we moved on again, and the pain was worse now. When I stopped to ease it, they hit me with their rifle butts, and the blows stung me deep, not only because of the pain but in the sudden realization that these short, simple farmers were not one bit willing to show any compassion. Finally two guards put their arms around me so I could lean my weight on them, and they literally dragged me along that footpath.

As we moved along the path, people passed us going in the opposite direction. I tried to gesture to them, build some rapport. I wanted them to see that I was human, not some kind of monster out of a war machine. I used the word *"ciao"* that passed for a greeting in Europe. Some nodded back to me. But a couple of them I greeted slapped my face in return. I was to find out later that *"ciao"* sounds like the Chinese word *"chou,"* which means dog.

A couple of hours later we arrived at what had to be a schoolhouse: there were blackboards in the room with math written on them in chalk. They had given me a little bit of sweetened tea from their thermos bottles to ease my thirst, but it hadn't helped much. Outside the schoolhouse they had dug a hole six feet deep and six feet long with a partial shelter over it. They made me get down into that hole, still bound, and I figured this was it. They were now going to shoot me, or, worse yet, bury me alive. But I really didn't care. I was totally dejected and numb from the shock of my wounds that kept nagging at me with steadily increasing pain.

I stayed in that hole for at least three hours, and people came from everywhere, it seemed, to get a look at me. Some were hostile, but most were simply curious and stared down at me like I was some rare species of jungle animal in a cage. To them, the war was something unreal out here in the country, since American bombing concentrated mostly on Hanoi. But the leaders worked them up anyway with yelling and chants, so that some of the crowd began to spit and throw dirt at me.

Then, without warning, they had me up out of the hole and up into the back of a truck. As we started out, I figured we had to be heading for Hanoi. I didn't relish the thought of what was to come there, but I was at least glad I could ride instead of walk. Some time later the truck stopped, and I was taken off and put into a tent in what appeared to be an army encampment. Once more I was on display. A lot of people came to look, including children. I tried communicating with one little boy, and his mother slapped me in the face. Then some of the leaders came in and began interrogating me in poor English. I gave them all I was supposed to and no more—name, rank, serial number, and date of birth.

Then it was back to the truck again, sometime around two or three in the morning. I rode next to a full fifty-five-gallon drum of gasoline which spilled over on me with every bump. I thought of escape a few times on that ride, but I knew I wouldn't get far with the wounds I had.

As we got closer to Hanoi, the treatment became rougher. Hanoi had felt the worst of the American bombing. And now and then a few people along the road would get into the truck when we stopped and kick my legs. I yelled in protest but nobody paid any attention, least of all my two guards in the truck with me. But that treatment was nothing compared to what I was in for from the North Viet military.

I arrived in the Hanoi Hilton, the main American prison camp, at about 5:30 that Sunday morning. I was put into a room which was small, windowless, and musty-smelling. I heard the iron gates clang shut behind me, and I settled down hoping to get a few hours of sleep, because right then my mind and body ached for rest. Instead an officer came in, read the camp regulations, and made the point that I was not to communicate with fellow prisoners. I felt some spark of elation in knowing that there were American prisoners here, and I thought maybe I'd get to see some of my friends who'd been shot down earlier. After a while the officer went out, and I stayed seated on the floor. I saw a big cockroach go by, about two inches long and sporting wings, of all things. There is nothing more grimly symbolic of what a man has to look forward to than a cockroach. But when they come that big and can fly as well as walk it's an even worse omen.

Then the interrogators were there again, and I tried to point out my injuries to them. They were unmoved. "You talk, medicine later," one of them said shortly. So they went to work trying to extract military information from me. When I wouldn't come through, they put me into the ropes, a treatment I was to know and dread in the long pull ahead. They tied my wrists tight, then pulled my arms high behind me, binding me so that my shoulder bones were ready to pop. Again they questioned. For forty-five minutes to perhaps more than an hour they kept me in the ropes, and the sweat ran off me in buckets as the pain in my shoulders reached the point of sheer agony. They loosened me for a few minutes to question me again; when I didn't give them anything, it was back into the ropes.

I pretended to pass out several times in hopes they would untie me and leave me alone. But they were wise to that. At times I would bite my shoulder hard to try to transfer the pain from one area to another. Then I began pounding my head against the wall, hoping for blood, something liquid to ease my terrible thirst. They finally brought in a bowl half filled with water with some greens floating in it; it wasn't much, but the thirty-minute respite I had to take it was everything. They gave me that meager food and water twice a day, mainly to keep me alive and conscious so they could continue their interrogations.

All the time the same questions were thrown at me asking about the Navy's new walleye missile, the television bomb, the new targets in Hanoi the Navy would be bombing. Sometime during all of that I lost control of my bowels and bladder, and the warmth of my urine felt strangely comforting. Finally, unable to take much more of the pain, I figured I had to tell them something, anything, to get relief. But it had to be phony. I would never tell them I was an A-6 pilot, the one plane that had penetrated Hanoi with devastating results. If they knew that, they would probably get really tough with me, though I couldn't imagine anything tougher than what I was presently experiencing. So I told them about the A-1 Skyraider plane, because it was not very sophisticated in its radar and electronic devices and not highly classified in our military. I knew that A-1, because I had flown over two thousand hours in it, so I could make it believable. They listened and asked me what my mission was in flying that plane, and I told them it was rescue operations. They were not that convinced, so they went back to asking again about the Hanoi bombing targets. I sensed then that they seemed more concerned for themselves in knowing those targets than in the big war effort. I gave them a few target areas down around the DMZ south, but they didn't want any of that.

For two days, to stay out of the ropes, I fed them phony information. On the third day they came in with a kneeboard with the name McDaniel on it. It was out of my downed A-6, and I was sure then they knew I was lying. Still I stuck to my story, that the kneeboard was out of the A-1 plane, not the A-6. They couldn't prove otherwise. All the time I was hoping that Kelly Patterson had been rescued and was not in the next room fabricating a story of his own that would not jibe with mine. If so, then it would indeed be hell for both of us.

Five days after torture, they let me out of the leg irons and threw me into an adjoining area outside that was called the wash area, where prisoners bathed or washed their clothes. It was only later that I could explain their sudden dismissal of me, when I found that the day I was shot down, Friday, May 19, was the worst day for our flights. We had lost seven aircraft that day. That meant more prisoners were coming in for torture, so they put me aside for a while to get at the new shoot-downs.

I was six hours in that wash area trying to get some sleep, trying to ignore the pain from the irons that had clamped hard on my ankles and the ropes. I had lost the use of my right hand. My right ankle was swollen from the one leg iron. I was glad for the reprieve from the torture, but I couldn't be sure when it would begin again. Eight hours later I was put into solitary confinement, and I began to get some sense of the horror of what was ahead of me now. Those "simple little farmers" in the hamlets who had captured me what seemed so long ago—they were long gone out of my mind. I knew I was up against a monstrous situation, against an enemy who seemed to take great satisfaction in inflicting pain, who performed like robots in doing so. The question I had to face now was: Could I take that kind of torture again? And, of course, the other question: Was it so important that I refuse to answer their questions anyway? In the hours and days ahead, I was to feel this nagging question even more strongly as I listened to the screams of my fellow pilots going through the same torture, some maybe even worse. I had more coming too; I knew it.

Yet I had taken the first round of agony without telling them anything they really wanted. Something had risen to the surface in me, some quality of resistance. From where? Was it my old athletic discipline? Was it the hating to lose, drilled into me early in life? Was it the military code I had followed for the past twelve years—the pride in sticking to it, no matter what? Was it my fragile faith in God? Maybe. I had to admit right then, however, that my faith in God had taken a nose dive back in the jungle when those Jolly Greens didn't show up and the Vietnamese home guard did instead. I really didn't know what faith I had that was strong enough to hold me in the future.

But I kept coming back to the big point: I *had* come through a very bad time, my initial baptism in torture. I had been shaken to the depths of my emotional and physical makeup. My mind was drained, and I had a hard time focusing on any given thought pattern for long. *Yet I had come through.* Though there was going to be more, maybe I could condition myself for it. I knew, too, that if I had to go into it again, I had to draw on what was available to help me. I knew that if I didn't find some resources to hold me, I was going to die—because I knew I wasn't going to tell them anything, and in that case all that was left was to die in those ropes in the end.

Right then I started to paw over the torn-up fragments of what I had left of myself, trying to pull them back into some kind of whole. I was conscious of how bad I smelled, and even the guard who brought me water had to keep his handkerchief over his nose. I hurt in every bone; to move was agony. What resources were there?

One thing I knew I had to have: communication with my own people here. I knew there were American flyers here like myself facing the same grim future and fearing the worst, either ending up telling what they did not want to tell or dying in the process of holding out. These were people like myself who wanted to live through this if at all possible. For us to do that, we had to communicate with each other, to let each other know that we were together, come what may.

Communication with each other, however, was the one occurrence that the North Vietnamese captors were taking the greatest pains to prevent. They knew, as well as I and the others did, that a man can stand more pain if he is linked with his own kind in that suffering. The lone, isolated being becomes weak, vulnerable. I knew then that I had to make contact, no matter what it cost, and this would be my first resource.

The next day, and God knew exactly my concern, I was taken to the wash area by my guard. When I came in, I heard two other men talking, and I could tell they were Americans because they were talking to each other in low tones, even though they were being monitored by a guard a few feet away. When their guard and mine moved off a bit, I took the chance and said, "Who are you?"

One of them answered, "You by yourself?"

"Yes," I said.

"We can't talk," the man replied shortly—which meant,

apparently, that any man in solitary confinement like me was forbidden any communication, and others were forbidden to try to communicate back.

Four days later I tried again in the same wash area. This time they asked me if I was alone, and I said no, because I had to break through. So they started talking very carefully to me, and one of them asked if I had the code.

"Morse code?" I asked.

"No, the camp code."

I knew then, for the first time since shoot-down, that there was a system of communication that was eventually to play a large part in holding me and hundreds of others together.

But as I took on a new sense of optimism about this, I had to have something else even more critical to my needs. I had to get out of solitary confinement and be with someone like myself. I had no idea how long my prison commanders would keep me isolated, but I knew that as long as I remained alone my strength and will would diminish. So I prayed, even in my feeble faith, that God would give me someone, because communications meant nothing unless there was someone close to talk to.

Then it happened. When they came to get me that day, fourteen days after shoot-down, I figured it meant going up for more torture. Instead they took me into another room called the Tet Room in the Little Vegas complex of the Hanoi Hilton. These "complexes" were groups of buildings in various places within the compound. The VC kept moving prisoners around to the various complexes in an attempt to break up the communications system. The Tet Room was small, maybe ten by twelve, and had two flat board bunks. The room was connected to another the same size by a narrow passageway or hallway between.

When I walked in I saw the man lying on the floor, and I knew he was critically wounded. His arms had open wounds from the wrists up to the elbows. He had a gash in his left thigh some eighteen inches long, seven to eight inches deep, where a two-pound piece of shrapnel had gone through.

The other leg was broken. His name was Lieutenant (jg) Bill Metzger. He had been shot down ten minutes before me.

We looked at each other as if we were each seeing an apparition. Metzger later was to tell me that when I walked in I looked like a man sixty-five years old, with boils all over my body, a dangling right hand, left leg dragging from the knee, and stooped over from my torture in the ropes. But as I looked at the handsome face of Bill Metzger, dark hair, clear blue eyes, twenty-five years of age, I suddenly realized the selfishness of my question of God when I was shot down: "God, why me?" Now, looking at Metzger, so helpless there, with wounds open and gaping, I said, "God, why *not* me?"

Metzger, as eager as I for contact, said, "Where have you been?" He was, I could tell, shocked by the way I looked.

I grinned, though it hurt, because in a way it was funny. After a bit I managed to pick him up and move him to the flat board bed we had there. It took all I had to do it, but I couldn't leave him on that floor with those wounds. After a while the guard came in and was surprised that I had managed to get Bill up on that bed, and even Metzger had to grin at the guard as if to say there was more going for us than he could add up.

I paused there and took stock. I somehow sensed now the purpose that God might have had for allowing me to be shot down. It wasn't perfectly clear, but I had to grab onto the possibility that I probably had something I could give to the others that was needed here. God knew I wasn't in good enough shape physically either right then to take on any such cause. But I realized at the same time that I had used what strength I had with Metzger, that it was more than I thought I had after all that torture, and that in the giving of it maybe I would get something back to keep myself going too.

At any rate, God gave me answers to my two prayers, though at the time I was not certain how it would all come out. First, though He had passed me over in my plea to get rescued out of that jungle, He now had given me a roommate, a big help in keeping my own sanity in this place. Second, He had given me knowledge of a communications system that could keep me in touch with others—which, I hoped, would keep my morale up.

But as I took heart about the possibility of communication, I had no idea that it was going to lead me to my darkest, longest night of terror.

4

Communicate—or Die

MEN FACED WITH THE HOPELESSNESS of a military prison and the uncertainty of what a day might bring from the enemy, surrounded by walls too high to look over, and confined to a small room with nothing to do but think and sink deeper into depression, soon become desperate to communicate with others. Morale was essential, and one of the keys to morale was to beat the enemy as often as possible in their attempts to keep us isolated or to force us to yield to their demands. What's more, it was imperative to communicate in order to know what others were going through in torture so the rest of us could be prepared for the exact kind of questions and the exact kind of torture we were to receive. More than that, we wanted to know from pilots shot down after us how the war was going and, more specifically, any news of our families.

I began immediately to figure out the system while in the Tet Room with Bill Metzger. Three pilots were put in with us in the first part of June; two of them were moved out, and the third, Major Tom Sterling of the Air Force, remained with us. Tom was from Texas, forty-two years old, had salt-and-pepper hair and a heavy torso which he never lost during all of his imprisonment, even though the food was abominable and there was not much of it. He was an easygoing, tranquil man, a personality I was to come to appreciate in the long months and years ahead when tempers would flare and we would turn on each other. He had two broken legs, one a simple fracture, the other a compound. He had been shot down in April and had managed to get medical treatment in exchange for making a propaganda tape for the Vietnamese which he made sure didn't amount to much. But Tom's feet, which had pointed outward naturally anyway, never did seem to be fitted on right since the North Vietnamese surgeons had worked on them. Many times he would stand looking down at them, wondering if the outward angle had been increased by five or six degrees. As a result, his walk was even more penguin in gait than usual, and sometimes his movements resembled the TV ad called the "Teaberry shuffle." We laughed at his concern about it—at least at those times when he was willing to laugh about it as well.

But when Tom joined us in the Tet Room he was not able to walk at all. I helped him to the showers when we were allowed to go and set him on a stool while I washed him down. Meanwhile, Bill Metzger's gaping wounds weren't improving. He never moved out of his bed, and the wounds would drain heavily, soaking through the clumsy bandages we had improvised. Sometimes the stench was unbearable. Many times, in my exasperation in not receiving medical care, I would yell to the guards the words *"Bao cao!"* (pronounced "bow-cow"). That meant we needed a guard who understood English so we could explain the critical need for medical attention. But most of the time the guards ignored it.

Finally, after persisting—the three of us yelling *"Bao cao!"* over and over again—we got the Vietnamese doctor, whom we had named Dr. Zorba. He was very polite, spoke crisp French, and showed real concern for Metzger's wounds. He said he should operate, but the camp commander refused permission. The next best thing he could do was try to close the wound in the leg, so he sewed it together with tobacco twine after laying on a white salve which was supposed to be an anesthetic but which did not seem to alleviate Bill's pain through it all. The tobacco "stitches" lasted a week and then broke apart. So Zorba came back and laid heavy metal clamps on the wound, hoping that would close it. Within a few days, the wound split open again under the clamps. All the time, Metzger lay in his flat board bunk trying not to show the pain. His clothes had been taken away, so he was in the nude all the time. In fact, he had very little of anything. He did have a towel, a small tin cup, and a half unraveled bamboo fan he used to keep the flies off the draining gashes in his leg and up along his left arm. He posed a pathetic figure in those early days, and he would be like that for ninety days before any improvement showed in his injuries, no thanks to the Vietnamese.

Meanwhile, I began to work on the communications system used by the other prisoners there in the Hanoi Hilton. I found out my first day with the camp commander that there were already established ways. He insisted, for example, that I not "write under plates, write notes and put them under toilet bowls, cough, sing, or tap on the walls." These, of course, were the exact methods the others were using.

Early in June I got the camp code from Ralph Gaither and Mike Cronin by talking to them in the wash room—which, of course, was forbidden. The guards caught us, and we were taken to interrogation immediately. There the interrogator, the one I was to come to know and dread the most, was a guard we called ONI—Operations Naval Intelligence—which meant he dealt only with Navy prisoners. We also called him Sweetpea, because he was so precise with the English. He began by saying, "Who are you living with? Or, shall I say, with whom are you living?" It was very important to him, even above anything else, that the usage be correct.

Now he simply told me to write down everything I had said to Gaither and Cronin. I said we weren't talking, that I had been conversing, or trying to, with a VC guard in the next room. Sweetpea laughed at the ludicrousness of that, and apparently it was since I was so naive that he let me go back to my room.

But I had the code, even though much later I was to find out that both Gaither and Cronin spent seventeen days in torture for their part in that. The code was simply designed around five rows of letters across and five rows of letters down. When anyone wanted to send anything on that code, he would tap on the walls the number of times that corresponded to the letters either up or down in that block. When hanging clothes, it was simply a matter of snapping a shirt to fit the code. When sweeping in the courtyard, the thumping of reed brooms in the dirt would tap out the same kind of code, moving up and down those rows of letters:

	1	2	3	4	5
1	A	F	L	Q	V
2	B	G	M	R	W
3	C	H	N	S	X
4	D	I	O	T	Y
5	E	J	P	U	Z

When we wanted to tap out a message, we would tap according to the vertical column first and then the horizontal line. If we wanted to say "VC," we would tap out five times meaning the column the letter V was in, pause, then one more tap indicating the top line. Then we would tap out one again, indicating the first column, pause, and then three more taps to indicate three lines down. It was cumbersome and confusing at first, but after a while it came to us easily. By abbreviating our communications we could say a lot just by the use of letters alone without the full words.

Still, I was to learn to use it the hard way. That same afternoon I was experimenting with it by tapping on the walls of our room, trying to get a message to the people next door. I got an answer, so I tapped out the name of my ship. While I was doing that, Bill Metzger happened to look down at a hole in the floor near the lower wall which was for ventilation and drainage, and saw a guard looking up at me, watching me busy at my work. The signal I had been getting from the other side of the wall—which I could not decipher until later—was a danger signal, warning me that a guard was near. Since I hadn't learned the complete communications repertoire yet, I was caught dead.

So I went back into interrogation, and Sweetpea was

there. He looked at me silently in an unnerving stare as if to say this was getting serious. Then he asked what I was pounding on the walls, and I told him it was Morse code, that I was practicing it.

"Why?" he asked.

I thought fast. "Because there is nothing else to do . . ."

Again, apparently considering my newness in the camp, he let me go back to my room, giving me two books to read, *Ho Chi Minh's Teaching* and *Guerrilla*. I tossed them on the floor by my bunk, never cracking a page, disgruntled with myself that I was so clumsy in my attempts to make contact with the others.

But I went on checking it out, learning all the various ways, besides tapping, for communicating. I learned that when in the courtyard, when we couldn't use the tapping business, one cough from another prisoner in the yard or the wash area meant danger; two coughs meant it was all clear; and four coughs meant "stand by," a message was about to come through. Sometimes we could communicate to someone nearby using our fingers, flashing one, two, five, or whatever, always tied in with the code in that horizontal and vertical block of letters.

I learned to hear the taps from the other side of our walls by devising methods of amplifying the sound. For instance, by placing the open end of my tin cup flush against the wall and putting my ear up close to the bottom of it as a "funnel," I could hear much more easily. Sometimes by placing my blanket in a doughnut shape up against the wall to serve similarly, I could hear much better.

But the word, in any case, in all of this was to play it carefully. If we were caught, it would go hard on us with the guards. We had no idea how far we could push the line with them on the issue, so very early I, along with the other prisoners, began to study them—their personalities, their points of weakness or strength or even compassion. If we were to succeed at all in maintaining our communications, in building a necessary togetherness, we had to know as much as possible about our captors. We began to sense that the Viets were stoic, hard to know, hard to read, and inconsistent. "The only thing consistent about the North Vietnamese," we would often say, "is their inconsistency." Whether that was a deliberate attempt to keep us off balance or their nature, we did not know; the main thing was that it frustrated us in our attempts to stay ahead of their intentions. A certain response one day on their part might indicate a pattern which would be totally contradicted the next day in the same situation. So we learned to accept that inconsistency as the danger we had to be aware of and live carefully around. There was also no pity, no compassion, no emotion at all; in fact, there was nothing in them to indicate they were dealing with human beings.

"I am here to give you your rations and bury you when you die," one of them told me at the very outset. That was a chilling portent of the kind of jailer we had to deal with. Maybe the inhumaneness was true of all captors in military prison camps; maybe if I had been in their place I would have had the same attitude. The point was, however, that there wasn't going to be much given to us in terms of humane treatment, and we had to prepare for that in the risks we took in communicating with each other.

Also, they seemed to feel inferior to us. Maybe that was only natural, since we did represent a superior war machine in terms of technology. It might have won some respect from them for us. Instead it built in them a kind of ruthlessness that became more and more sadistic: it bred a heavy-handed superiority and made them sensitive in odd ways. For instance, we were never allowed to sit before them and cross our legs—that was a pose of relaxation and, perhaps, insubordination. When we sat in front of them, we had to sit very straight, both feet on the floor. We could never stand with our backs to them, which was interpreted as defacing them. When we did sit down, we could never sit above them; we must always be lower than their position. Some of that might have been cultural sensitivity, but the intent was more than that here. They were out to do everything they could to make us lower than they were. They made certain we were aware of the fact that we were the enemy, and they were going to treat us accordingly. And that meant at times we were made to feel like animals—and maybe I couldn't blame them for feeling that way toward us, but the devastating pressure and pain meted out in that kind of situation was more and more difficult to bear with each passing day.

What all this meant was that if we were to stay alive under that treatment we had to study them continually, test them, find any possible point that we could exploit for ourselves or that would allow us a margin to play with in communication with the others. So we began to peg them with names that best suited their personalities and physical appearance or summed up their attitudes toward us.

Besides ONI or Sweetpea—we were coming to know him very well in the torture room for his exactness in everything, whether it was English or the nature of the torture—we had another guard named The Rat. When I first met him, he seemed concerned for the fact that I was losing weight and asked, "Do you eat, Moc?" ("Moc" was the nickname they had given me.) I almost laughed at that, because there wasn't much to eat. Then he added, "You must eat, keep up strength." I thought maybe The Rat was sincerely compassionate underneath, but later I was to find that he was anything but that in the torture room. I sensed that his concern for my weight and strength was purely to make certain I wouldn't pass out too early in torture before giving in.

We had another guard named Slug or The Frog, who also did a lot of the torturing. He was all muscles and loved to flex them in front of us. He had no heart at all—and he made a point of communicating that to us. The only way to explain him was "savage," and that said it all.

There was WTG, the World's Tallest Gook, who at five feet ten inches actually towered over his shorter countrymen. His hang-up was punctuality and anything he asked us to do was followed by a "Queekly!" He served on the torture team called "the goon squad," and we knew he couldn't be pushed far.

And there was Soft-soap Fairy, who was in the top

echelon of the political system of the prison program. Whenever he came around, something good was going to happen to us. He never showed up in the torture. He knew English well, had a friendly face, but we knew he was as dangerous, if not more so, than the others, because he knew what the intent of the torture was—either to gain military information or to get propaganda tapes.

Another guard we named B. O. Plenty or The Elf. Peculiarly, he was always fishing in the open sewer pond, which we called Lake Fester, where we dumped our waste. He was always anxious to tell us some new information as to what was happening in the war or if the food was going to get worse or better. He seemed to think this gave him status above the others. He was always status-conscious, and his uniform had been deliberately laundered over and over until it was white instead of khaki.

Then there was Ashley Asthmatic, so named because he was always coughing and therefore we could always hear him coming—which meant he never did catch us at anything. He had a round face, an easygoing manner, and perhaps slightly more compassion for us than the others had. Yet when he was told to torture us, he did so, no questions asked. He had one favorite term he used on all of us: *"Dummkopf."* "Why you do this?" he would often say to me, and then add, *"Dummkopf?"*

Another guard who distracted us considerably in the torture area was the one we called The Bug, because without warning his right eyeball would roll up into his head and disappear.

The camp commander we called Rabbit, for he had buck teeth, fat cheeks, and big ears. He was on a constant ego trip and insisted that "we will control you even if you ever do get back to the United States." He was a master psychologist and sometimes would open the peephole in our door and just stare at us. It was unnerving, because we didn't know which one of us he would decide to pull out for torture.

The building officer we called Spot, because he had brown spots all over his neck. He was one of the main interrogators. Now and then we could see him from our ceiling vent, walking back and forth on the porch of his quarters practicing his interrogation. I never looked into his face, because there was something diabolical there that gave me the creeps. I always kept my eyes six inches above his head just to avoid that chilling eyeball-to-eyeball confrontation. I finally made this a practice with the other interrogators too.

Then there were others like Jawbone, who had a horse face and a protruding jawline—he was just plain ruthless. And we had Hanoi Fats in the Hilton who was thirty pounds overweight and knew how to throw it around in torture.

Dr. Zorba was the one medical man we respected because of his attempt to show concern and give us halfway decent treatment. When we bowed to him, which was a rule for us whenever any of them entered, he would bow politely back. Unfortunately, he was replaced by another medic we called Seal Beams, because he wore very thick-lensed glasses. Later we got another medical orderly we named Tonto, because, like Zorba, he was concerned for our wounds. He was young, meticulous, hard-working.

All these guards, and more—there were thirty or forty of them in the bigger complexes of the Zoo and the Zoo Annex—had their peculiarities in looks or in attitudes which sometimes tipped us off as to what to expect. All of them, however, had one task: break us by whatever means available.

And yet, oddly enough, they gave us, unintentionally, some sources of humor too. For instance, WTG, the World's Tallest Gook, commented one day, "You Americans would complain even if we shot you with a silver bullet!"

At another time, the camp commander, Rabbit, was questioning a Navy enlisted man named Hegdahl about the size of the ship he had sailed. Hegdahl was an unusual type in our camp in that he was not a pilot or officer. He had fallen over the side of his ship and was picked up by North Vietnamese patrol boats. The camp commanders figured he was a CIA man deliberately dropped over the side to get information. On this day, then, Hegdahl said he didn't know the length of his ship or couldn't remember. So Rabbit told him he would walk off the paces across the compound and Hegdahl was to stop him when he thought it was about the length of his ship. So Rabbit walked it off, and Hegdahl signaled to him when he thought it was about right—though Hegdahl was as inaccurate as he dared to be—and then Rabbit took a tape measure and measured the distance. When he came back toward Hegdahl, Hegdahl asked, "How big?"

"Military secret," Rabbit said bluntly, and that was that.

Then later, when Captain Bill Austin was shot down, he was led into our camp and to our room, blindfolded, pushed along by a guard we called J.C. When he pushed Austin into our room, he yelled, "Bow!" to us. This was required of us every time a guard walked in, but Austin thought he was being ordered to do so. So he did, and that put him in a bent-over position toward J.C., the worst of insults, and J.C. promptly gave him a boot in the behind and sent him sprawling. We couldn't help but laugh at that, after the guard had gone.

One of the more peculiar guards in terms of attitude was Little Caesar, so named because of the way he would strut around and play the big wheel. He took a fancy to Bill Metzger for some reason, sometimes just watching him from the door a long time. We thought perhaps he had a soft spot for Bill's good looks. One day after watching Bill a long time, he said, "Handsome is as handsome does." And he went away. None of us knew what he meant by that—if he was irritated at Bill for being handsome or simply playing with words. We laughed at it, because there was so little to laugh at; but at the same time we tried to figure the hidden meaning, not knowing if we should laugh or not.

At other times Little Caesar, with no warning, would fling open the door of our cell and shout, "You will be here until the cows come home!" He was always trying to pick up American idioms and would take delight at throwing them at us. Another time Little Caesar, who had probably rehearsed for a long time another line that he had read in the newspapers, shouted at us, "Why doesn't Lyndon Johnson take it on the chop and go home?"

Sometimes there wasn't much humor in the remarks or the acts, but we squeezed all we could out of what came our way. There really wasn't that much to draw on. In torture there was nothing funny at all. No jokes; no compassion even. Only once did I hear of a guard who refused to torture any more Americans. Having done enough of it, he finally jumped up and ran out of the room screaming at the officer that he would not be a part of it again. But, rare as those incidents were, we took hope that maybe not all of our captors were totally ruthless, totally sadistic.

Yet it was that ruthless streak in our guards that plagued us day after day. For instance, they raised dogs to eat, but used them for sport as well. They would chase a dog with clubs and bricks until the poor animal was driven to total exhaustion. Then they would kill it. Running the dog mercilessly, they said, was to tenderize the meat. But what unnerved us even more was when they would take a dog into a foxhole in the camp and torture it to death for the sheer pleasure of inflicting pain. The practice of blinding their pigs to make them more docile or dousing rats with gasoline and lighting them for the sheer sport of it was, again, peculiar to their own kind of life. But it got to us, because we did not know how far that "sporting" streak in them would carry over to us in the torture room. If life, even animal life, was no more to them than that, was our value much higher?

We found some of that sporting streak would be directed at us too. Once Tom Sterling found a nail and kept it in his room; just to possess something was helpful to morale. WTG, the World's Tallest Gook, found it on Tom and made him stand on those very bad legs for six hours with his arms over his head. It was a painful time for him in his physical condition, and I asked WTG if he would let me stand for Tom. He screamed at me to be quiet. All because of a nail. But that's the way it was going to be—there were no small things to them. We had carried the war to them, and we had to pay in whatever means they decided on.

Sometimes this sporting streak took the form of "free-lance" harassment. Some of these incidents were not necessarily approved by the camp commander. One night, when the American air raids were heavy around us, the guards got drunk and took three American prisoners out of one of the rooms. One of them never did come back, and we were pretty sure he had been tortured to death.

Sometimes they would wake us up in the middle of the night and make us march around our room for an hour. At other times, if they so much as heard our bed boards squeak as we turned in our sleep, they would throw open the door and accuse us of trying to communicate.

Between all of those "free-lancing" acts of harassment was the North Vietnam radio that came on over the camp P.A. every morning at five. For an hour we would hear all kinds of wildly exaggerated statistics of American war casualties. Once there was an interview with an American father who had lost his son in Vietnam and who, as a result, condemned the American involvement. At another time, the "news" reported that an American pilot had gone AWOL and run off to Sweden. We tried to ignore the continual propaganda over that station, and we managed most of the time. But after a while, as the days grew longer, that radio would dig deeply into our resolve and chafe on our nerves.

Meanwhile, there were others in the camp going through their own hours of torture. For one week I was assigned the job of washing the other prisoners' clothes, and many of the ragged uniforms coming in were soaked or stained with urine or excrement. This meant a lot of men were catching hell in the Quiz Room, and it all said to me that we had a long row to hoe here.

Strangely enough, there was another trait the North Vietnamese had, besides their sadism: the need to save face. This is a common Oriental trait, but it came out even more in the prison environment. Though not conscious of their inconsistencies of behavior in general, our guards were very aware of any contradiction they might detect in themselves in terms of their self-image. If their propaganda said they ran their prison "humanely and with compassion," they would oddly become anxious if we began to show signs of deterioration in health. For us to look poorly violated their self-image, even though they masterminded the forces that broke us down. If a prisoner would not or could not eat, for instance, they would go to great lengths to pour nourishment into him, even to inject blood plasma, because his weakness contradicted their propaganda and made them lose face. I did not know how this trait was to work for our benefit at all, but I tucked it away in my mental inventory with the others just in case there was something in it that could be used later.

In all of this, we simply had to take each day and move with the schedule and the routine, looking for our opportunities to communicate with others. Every day started with the morning gong at 5 A.M.—6 in the winter—and we would get up and make our bedrolls, do some exercising in the room, and be ready at eight for whatever the camp commander had for us in the way of work activities.

At about that time, the guard would come in and we would dump out our toilet bowls. Each room of three or four men had a two-gallon toilet bowl for urinating and defecating. Sometimes we would have one man in our room go and dump it; at other times, we would set it outside our door and one man would be assigned to pick up all the bowls and empty them. That finished, we would go work in the garden, sweep the courtyard, or wash our clothes, all of which afforded us communication opportunities.

At about ten we would get our first "meal," which broke nearly twenty hours of fasting—but which really didn't break it by much. It was a watery soup with a little rice. This meager food made us more tense, more conscious of our dwindling energy, more aware of how small our chances of survival were. With this demoralizing aspect of our lives, our motivation to communicate was often lessened. Food became our constant preoccupation—in our dreams, in our conversation. It also became the focal point for many instances of breakdown in discipline.

After twenty minutes for the meal, the guard would collect the bowls and have one of us assigned to go out and put them on the dish rack, unwashed, outside. At night the rats would come down and have a field day licking out those bowls. Just knowing the next meal would be served in those same bowls made some of the men sick. Others did, in fact, get seriously sick from the contamination. It wasn't until a year later in the Zoo Annex that we were able to get our demand for washing the bowls after meals cleared with the camp commander.

From 11:30 to 1:30 was siesta, and during this time we did our serious communicating. The guards were relaxed, knowing we would be napping anyway. At this time we would write notes. We found that, by mixing the brick dust that collected under our beds with water and using a bamboo stick from our brooms, we could write fairly well on the stiff onionskin toilet paper. Sometimes we used dried-out cigarette packages. We stuck these notes to the indented place in the underside of our toilet bowl, and when the man picked it up for dumping he would find it. We called this our "pony express" system, and it worked well. Though the guards knew we were doing this, and pulled surprise inspections now and then to catch us, we risked it anyway, because the need to get word to another room was far more important than the possible penalty for getting caught.

And of course there were other ways to communicate too: pounding on the walls, thumping the signals in the dirt with our brooms, and using coughs, hand signals, and clothes snapping.

Any time between 2 and 4 P.M. we had our second meal of the same soup. Then the doors were locked, and we settled down, knowing there would be no more quizzes for the day. And that opened those long evening hours, when we thought the most about our families, so much so that we had to find things to do or sink into total depression.

But in these hours I would continue to think of ways to communicate. It was during this time that the American bombing raids were heavy and coming closer to our camp.

Every night when they came over we were ordered to get under our beds. Tom and Bill could not, of course, because of their wounds. But on this night in particular, the raid came, and I went under my bed and had a good view of the passageway that led to the other room. While lying there, I saw another prisoner down that passageway crawl under his bed, so I got his attention and began communicating with him. I could tell he had been tortured, and I read his lips, which mouthed, "Where am I?"

I mouthed back that he was in the Hanoi Hilton. I gave him all three of our names and found that his was Jerry Gerndt. I didn't see him after that, but I was again elated that I could communicate with another prisoner. Even a brief encounter did a lot to pick up my morale, as it did for the others.

But, in taking these chances to make contact, I was always aware of the penalty for getting caught. Yet I feared isolation more than the possibility of torture. Still, I tried to play it carefully with the guards, and I thought I knew the limits for pushing it. As it turned out, I really didn't. On the night of September 12, after Metzger, Sterling, and I had moved up to the Thunderbird Room—which was built the same as the others and was an attempt again by the VC to break up the communications pattern we had with the other rooms in Little Vegas—I was out in the courtyard with the broom, and I moved down to sweep under Ron Mastin's door a few rooms down from my own. Ron had been put into a room by himself, solitary confinement, for six months, and the VC were trying to break him down. As I went by his door, he reached out his hand under the door and touched my toe. I stopped, strangely moved by the gesture of an American prisoner this starved for companionship.

But the guard saw it and jumped in immediately. He pushed me out of the way, so Ron would not be able to see me, then charged inside and confronted Ron. He checked Ron's knees first and saw dirt on them where he had kneeled down by the door, and he accused Ron of taking communication from me. But Ron, thinking quickly, denied it and said he was merely doing knee pushups. The guard ranted some more, but he seemed convinced. Yet he took me to the camp commander anyway, and I was thrown into the washroom and there blindfolded and put into irons. I could not see or move, nor was I allowed to sleep for thirty-six hours. Sometimes the guards would come in and spit at me or cuff me about and ask me what I had said to Mastin.

Finally they let me out, and I returned to my room and my companions again, smelling terrible from having to eliminate in my pants and getting those looks from them that said I ought to wise up about how far I pushed the VC in violating the communications rules; at the same time, however, I could tell they were also wondering how it was I could come out of that kind of punishment, return to the room, and begin planning my next move in communicating the code.

The fact was I didn't know why or how I could keep pushing myself either, especially when my captors were watching me more closely, knowing I was taking risks with the rules. Maybe I would have done differently if I had known how long I was going to be locked up inside the North Vietnamese prison system. If I had known that I had a six-year prison term and no more, maybe I would have played it more safe and cool, content to knock off my days until my time was up. But it was because I didn't know the length of my stay that every day became a challenge for me to stay alive; and to do that I had to find ways to outwit the enemy. All of this meant I had to have some belief in my success, some belief that I could beat the system each day and that, if I stayed with it long enough, I could live and one day be free. This attitude was to become one of my mainstays in the long months and years ahead, and, though I had not planned it, became a contagion that spread later on in the Zoo and the Zoo Annex where I was to spend most of my time in prison.

Where did that optimism come from? I knew it was not innate; nobody is really born an optimist. Considering that optimism does not normally flourish in the conditions of a military prison, where torture is the order of the day, it had to be a quality that had been deeply ingrained over time, a product of childhood and young adulthood. And yet, looking over those years, I figured I didn't have that much optimism input either, certainly no more than anyone else.

Maybe it was my background of athletics again, because I knew how much a positive attitude meant in terms of competition. I knew that an optimistic attitude about winning was essential to individual performance.

Yet I remember, too, the day my father died when I was a junior in college, and I went home to face my mother, who had nothing now, materially or otherwise, except what faith in God she had learned to lay hold of in the hard years as a sharecropper's wife. I wondered what she was going to do. There were five children still at home, two of them preschoolers. It would be a year before I could finish college and I thought I should drop out and get to work to help out. My mother would have none of that; it was her dream, as well as my father's, that I would get my education. When I asked her bluntly what she was going to do about making a go of it, she said calmly, assuredly, "Where there's a will, there's a way."

That seemed far too simple and idealistic a statement to me in the light of the facts. She was forty-seven years old and had to face up to finding her way out into the world to get a job after all those years. How could she work at anything outside and still keep the family together? How could she find the strength to do it all? It was going to be a long year before I finished college.

But I had underestimated her own courage and the strength the Lord was prepared to give her. She did find a job, as matron in a school for retarded children. She was responsible for thirty children in one of the units there, and I always wondered how she could take a job like that after raising so many of her own. But not only did she work at it, she even brought those children home many times just to give them the atmosphere. For her, the situation was there to face, and she faced it, fully confident that the Lord would provide whatever it took to make it each day. Even after I finished college and began sending money to her to help out, she never gave up that job.

So, for my mother, there were no simple little spiritual platitudes. She believed in what God could do and stuck by it. It was a lesson I never forgot, and it made a solid impression on me.

Later, when I was visiting the home of my father-in-law, a Baptist minister and a Bible teacher, I picked up Norman Vincent Peale's book *The Power of Positive Thinking*. The very same element of optimism my mother declared was expanded in that book. It was an optimism rooted in God's control of events and also in the God-given ability of every man to rise above his circumstances.

I was still a bit dubious about the sweeping possibilities of that simple truth, so in 1965 I decided to test it myself. I wanted to quit smoking, because I knew it was doing me no good. But, like all smokers, I couldn't kick the habit on my own strength alone; I always felt I needed a cigarette. I therefore grabbed on to the *positive* attitude that said I could quit, if I wanted to. So I asked God to help me and sat down with a sheet of paper and wrote what was good about smoking and what was bad. Soon the bad list far outweighed the good, and I determined that every day had to be a positive assurance to God and then to myself that I could lick this habit that could enslave me and maybe in the end destroy me.

I did quit smoking. Part of it was my facing each day with an optimistic view about overcoming it and the self-conviction that I didn't need to be enslaved by any habit or attitude that was not good for me. The other part was the belief that God would provide for me what strength I needed to make the day count for good to Him and to myself.

As I grew older in the faith, I came to realize that optimism was solidly rooted in faith in God—the optimism that worked, that is—and any attempt to build up a positive attitude apart from faith could only carry me so many miles. Believing in God's positive attitude toward me, that He wanted the highest good for me, was the only way I could face each day with confidence.

But, up until now, the options of life or death never hung so obviously in the balance. As I lay in my bunk that night staring at the mesh of my mosquito net and counting the holes down each side, I had to face the question: If I were to die tomorrow, could I face it with a smile? I remember Dorothy asking me, before I left for Vietnam, if I were ready to die. She really meant, Was my soul right with God? I said no. Why had I said that? Surely my commitment to Christ back there in college should have settled that? Maybe that's not what I meant when I said no? Maybe what I meant was that I was not ready to die in terms of giving up my life yet, that I would somehow outwit the enemy and stay alive? No matter how I looked at it, the question loomed up larger now as the possibility of dying was coming closer every hour. No, there was something, some part of my spiritual life not yet complete, and the question was posing a challenge to that area, though I could not fathom what it could be, until finally another question, almost as big as the other, rose up in my mind: If I had to face tomorrow in the torture room, when death would *not* come, when the pain would be so bad that death would be easier, would I smile then?

I didn't know. I should be able to as a Christian and as a man. I felt uneasy. Was I not ready to meet God? Was I not prepared to take whatever was coming and hang on in the strength Christ could give me in that hour? I didn't know how much torture I could take. No man really knew; but God surely knew how much I could stand. Right then I had to lay hold of Him, to renew my confidence in Him to control whatever came to the very end. But as the night wore on, and I thought of the ropes and irons, I began to sweat. I prayed that God would not let me suffer that again. I prayed for strength on the one hand and reprieve on the other. I knew I was faltering, so I prayed that, if He did intend for me to go through it, He not allow to die out in me the will to resist, to remain positive through it all, to stay confident in what He was going to accomplish in me and through me. I had to have that positive outlook if I was going to hold on. At the same time, I settled the other major factor too—I made sure right then my soul was right with Him if death was, in fact, His purpose for me.

I felt better for that, but I knew there was still something not yet in place, something perhaps that could only come with future events. It was not easy praying to undo that uncertainty. I was to do a lot of praying about it in the long nights ahead, because, even though I had peace about my soul if death were waiting for me, I still needed to be sure of myself just to stand up to each day when everything said it made no sense—and the need, too, to get that confidence in the Scripture in *Romans* 8:28 which said, "All things work together for good to them that love God." How easy to say that in the ordered world, the routine world outside, the world of, for the most part, easy days, no real threats, no sense of death or awful pain hanging over every minute! But I had to hang onto it here, because I was sure this was where God wanted to test it for me and in me for His own purposes.

Communicate or die, then, was the positive cry for me. But this decision had its painful complications too. I could not lose my will to communicate, to resist, to stay alive. God surely did not want me to lie down and play dead. If there was something to be lived in this sordid atmosphere of pain, then I had to live it. To abandon hope, the possibility of survival, meant I would lose possession of myself, my own worth, my own self-identity. In that case, the North Vietnamese had won—their intent was to destroy finally that sense of worth we all needed to hang on to. If I lost, then I was reduced to what the VC said all Americans, even Christian Americans, had to come to in the end: disillusionment with God, country, and the image of self, all of which led to hopelessness and despair. So every day was a battle to stay alive in a hopeless situation and resist my captors' attempts to exploit my weaknesses and break me. I sensed that to give in to them was to surrender a big chunk of what God was trying to instill in me. My tools for defense and offense were few, but I had to use them to the fullest.

Only time could tell, it seemed. Had I known then that six years of lying under that hole-pocked mosquito net were ahead of me, six years of mulling over those same thoughts every night, of sweating in the contemplation of torture, of fearing the loss of will, faith, and hope, I am not sure I could have held on. But God in His mercy was keeping that from me.

All I had was tomorrow then, and maybe that was the very height of optimism. Well, then, I would make tomorrow count for something—and on that I finally found sleep.

5

The Will and the Way

BUT THE TOMORROWS in a North Vietnam prison are not always the same and certainly not always so easy to approach. After that September torture, which proved that the guards were not going to fool around if they caught me communicating again, I realized it was going to be more difficult making the attempt. In fact, the camp commander made it plain that, if I tried it, I would be shot.

To further discourage any communication, we were moved out of the Hanoi Hilton in October to a new prison complex called the Zoo Annex. I hoped, in my typically optimistic way, that I would be allowed some reprieve from the interrogations and the torture. Meanwhile, before moving, we took on a new roommate, Air Force Captain Bill Austin, who was six-three, sported a blond crewcut, and hailed from South Carolina. He was an excellent storyteller—he knew all the major American authors—and his talent was to become a major asset for us in the months ahead when the days and nights became long and gloomy.

The move to the Zoo Annex was designed to break up our communications system in the Hilton. The seventeen moves I made during my six years were motivated by the same intent. The VC thought that, being surrounded by new men, some of whom did not have the code, and in a less conducive environment, we would be kept in isolation. Fortunately, in moving to the Annex, the daily schedule was the same, so we could at least work in familiar time blocks.

But the Annex had its peculiar and formidable barriers to communications, as we were to find out. It was a three-acre area locked in all around by a fifteen-foot wall. It was once a French film storage area, and when we were working in the garden we would often dig up yards of film and sometimes cans of it from the old days. The compound comprised five main prison buildings, each divided into two separate cells housing anywhere from four to nine men. When the nine men were crammed into the seventeen-by-twenty-one room, there was hardly space to sleep, let alone move around. In one corner of the compound, opposite the prison shacks, was the Quiz Room. In the middle of the compound was Lake Fester, where all of our waste was dumped and where B. O. Plenty did his fishing.

The rooms in the Annex were laid out much differently from the Tet and Thunderbird rooms in the Hanoi Hilton. Two doors separated us from the outside courtyard. The inner door had a small peephole for the guards to look in on us—and which we used, when the guards weren't around, to look out. To see anything through the door, however, the outer door had to be open, which was not often. The outside courtyard was twenty by twenty and hemmed in by a twelve-foot wall of brick. In that courtyard was a wash area, a well, a dish rack, and a two-hole john.

Inside the rooms the nature of the building's construction posed a problem unlike that which we had so far encountered. The walls were nineteen inches thick, made of cement, with an eight-inch void in between. Trying to tap the code through that barrier would be next to impossible. That left us with the alternative systems that were within possibility—using the brooms when we swept down the outer courtyard or main walkway and the toilet bowl "pony express." We began to use these with some effect, but since the code was not always readily understood with new men and since the pony express was being monitored more closely by the guards, we decided to try drilling through those courtyard walls to make a hole through which we could pass a note.

This was risky business, of course, because we were in the open in that courtyard, and trying to dig a hole in the mortar was not something we could do under cover. But we went ahead anyway, because the need to know who was with us there—and the need to reassure the new men, in particular, that we weren't copping out in the torture—was essential. Again, beyond that, was our own need to get new information on the war, and, we hoped, some news about our families.

So we drilled those holes in the courtyard walls, one man watching for the guards at all times and giving that one quick cough when danger was near. Being allowed out for only an hour a day did not give us much time, so we tried to make it count. We used an empty toothpaste tube or an old rusty nail to dig in the mortar. It took us more than two weeks to get through that mortar between the bricks. When we finished with it, we realized that the VC could spot it easily enough and watch for any notes coming through. So we decided to cut another hole down low on the wall; it would not be so obvious, and it could become our main drop.

In order to avoid exposing the men on the other side of the wall when they checked their "mailbox" too often for a possible note, we rigged a signal on the clothesline that ran across our courtyard walls. We put a piece of bamboo stick from our brooms on the line when there was a note in the hole; that way, all the man on the other side had to do was look up at that line now and then and know whether to check for a drop.

When we first came to the Annex, I set about numbering the rooms in each building for easier identification. This way we could keep track of who was moving to where. When new shoot-downs came in, we would need to know where they were housed, since it was they who would have the most up-to-date information for us.

As we began using this note-passing system through the courtyard walls, we found out that next door to us were four men who called themselves The Four Winds. Diagonally across from us beyond the five-foot walkway that separated the compounds, in Room 6, were the O-4's, meaning they were all Air Force majors or Navy lieutenant commanders. The room directly across the walkway from us, Room 5, housed a team of younger officers who called themselves The Kids. One night the VC moved them all around, as was their custom, and The Kids landed in the compound directly behind us, Room 2. We found out that four new shoot-downs had been moved into the diagonal compound, Room 6. So we started communicating to Room 6 by the note method, but we received no response. After a couple of days we started picking loose mortar from our courtyard walls and tossing it over into their courtyard to get attention. We literally bombarded them with pieces of brick, so much so that our courtyard wall looked as if it were ready to topple in. Still no response. We were to find out later that they wanted to send a note to us but were not sure how far they could push the guards.

This went on for three or four days with no answer, and I began to wonder who was over there. One day I decided to take the chance, and I climbed on top of our courtyard door, exposing my head and shoulders to any guards around, and took a quick look over their wall. No doubt about it, they were Americans—and, judging by the newness of their POW clothes, they were new shoot-downs.

Now we began to get a little irritated by their refusal to link up with our communications and "invitation" to start responding. So that fourth night I wrote a note on toilet paper and, figuring we ought to ease their tension, wrote: "WELCOME TO THE HANOI AIRMAIL CLUB." We told them how to write back to us, how to stick the message in their courtyard wall for pickup, and so on. We signed it THE FEARSOME FOURSOME to encourage them to take the chance.

In these notes we tossed over to them, we told them the signals that would precede our tossing them a message. We would cough loudly first, then throw up a towel in the air above the courtyard wall so they could see it. They would, in turn, throw up a towel acknowledging they were ready. So we threw up ours and saw theirs—all the time the guard, WTG, was watching what must have appeared to be a rather peculiar way to find amusement. We also managed to toss the note at the right time—when WTG was not looking. But, even with all that elaborate method of communicating, we still received no response.

We therefore drafted another note—and this was six or seven days later, by which time we were exasperated, because we were risking our necks with the VC. In this third note I wrote: "IF YOU ARE A COMMANDER OR A COLONEL, OR ABOVE, WE WOULD APPRECIATE HEARING FROM YOU . . . BUT IF YOU ARE A MAJOR OR A LIEUTENANT COMMANDER, OR BELOW, THEN GET OFF YOUR BUTT AND WRITE." In our room, of course, we had a major and a lieutenant commander, so we were in line.

Even then it wasn't until after another major move had been made that we found out who was in that compound—Major Ken Fleenor, Major Ray Vissotzky, Lieutenant Commander Jim Hickerson, and Lieutenant Commander Ed Estes. They had prepared a note to deliver to us but had hung onto it for days, not sure how to pass it or what the risk was to them. When it did come through much later, it was signed, of all things, THE FEARFUL FOURSOME! We had a good laugh over that one.

Later on, others would get laughs on me too. Some months afterward I had asked some new shoot-downs if they had any news about my wife. Commander Ned Shuman came back with: "WIFE DOING WELL . . . DRIVING AROUND IN A PINK CADILLAC WITH LEOPARD-SKIN UPHOLSTERY." My first reaction was a kind of jolt, and it was Ned's turn to laugh. When I realized Dorothy was not the type, I laughed too.

But we were convinced that note-dropping through the walls was probably not the best means to communicate here in the Zoo Annex. It took too long and exposed us too easily to the guards. One day we were in the room thinking about everything and anything; but all the time my mind was flitting around with how we could find a better way to make contact. I checked that room again: we had floor vents, those thick walls, and in the ceiling I noticed, as I had many times, four vents, each about eighteen inches in diameter. On top of each of these vents was barbed wire to keep us from trying to squeeze out. The more I thought about it and discussed it with the others, the more I thought that maybe we could get that wire off. For days we worked at it, lifting each other up on shoulders, until after a couple of weeks of chipping away at it we got the wire loose.

We then made our first move to take a look, squeezing our heads and part of our shoulders out easily. Up there we had a commanding view of the compounds, plus the villages outside the walls. We also found out we could squeeze up through that hole and get out—and, if we wanted to risk it, move across the roof and enter the small attic of the room next door. In our eagerness to do something daring to take our minds off the boredom and the depression, we played with the idea of exchanging roommates by means of that vent. It was an audacious, wild thing, and could cost us plenty if we got caught. But it seemed a beautiful way to "beat" the enemy, so we decided to try it on Sunday night. Sunday was a day when the guards relaxed and hardly ever came near our rooms. We set the toilet bowl out early in the morning, and the food was simply set inside the outer door. All the guard did was count bodies at night from the peephole in the door, and in the poor light he would never know who was who.

That night we pulled it off, and we laughed about it most of the night like kids who had tied a bell around the cat's neck while he slept. On Monday morning, we were all back in our places, but the sheer exhilaration of pulling that caper off lifted our morale as well as our adrenalin. In fact, Bill Austin got heady on the experience and wanted to go out every night and prowl around the compound. We finally vetoed that as too risky, convincing him that there was nothing to see out there at night that we couldn't see during the day.

But finding that ceiling vent open to us also added the

possibility of another dimension in communication across the compound. When I moved over to Room 7 of the Annex on March 28, 1968, with Tom Sterling—Metzger and Austin, whom we were to pick up again later, having been shifted to a room behind us—I figured a way then to make it count. We picked up two new roommates, Major Al Runyan, who came over from the Zoo, a prison complex right in back of us which we didn't know existed until then. Along with him came Major Bob Bagley and Lieutenant Commander Lee Hyatt. Later came four more, all of whom were in that diagonal compound we tried to get the response from—Lieutenant Commander Ed Estes, Lieutenant Commander Jim Hickerson, and Major Ray Vissotzky. The fourth man, Major Ken Fleenor, was from Bowling Green, Kentucky, a good golfer, very talkative, and a bad loser—like me. We were to have our days ahead battling each other in week-long chess games.

While in Room 7 with these men, one day I decided that there had to be a way of communicating to rooms across the compound through those ceiling vents. While out in the courtyard for our daily hour of fresh air, I went into the john that was right up against the other courtyard wall and began digging into the mortar with my empty toothpaste tube. I made sure there was one of my fellow prisoners standing guard, and for forty-five minutes, trying to ignore the smells in that small cubicle, I dug away at that mortar. After three weeks of this, I finally got through with a peephole big enough to see the vent in the building across the walkway. But it was the lower third of the vent that came into view and not the upper—which meant we couldn't see anything flashed from there. So I tried once more, digging a little higher this time, and two weeks later broke through; that put the hole right on the vent. It was five weeks of digging in that mortar, but it was worth it.

We passed the word over to that building that their vent was in view and they could flash the code from their vent with a pot cover or hand signals. To make sure we knew when to receive the signal from them, we asked them to put a broom in their vent when they were ready to communicate, and we would do the same. Since our schedules were different in the courtyard and getting into the john and that peephole, it was necessary to get our times straight.

When the other prisoners were informed that we had contact with the ceiling vent across the way through our john, we were able to bring all seventy-two prisoners into a workable and even more effective means of communicating.

Also, I found that the view through the ceiling vents opened to the Zoo directly behind us, beyond the fifteen-foot wall that separated the two prison complexes. When I looked out I could see the building directly behind, called the Garage. This was important, because later, when I was to be moved into the Garage, I would know the direction of the room I had been in while in the Annex and could set up a type of communications system which did not exist with the Zoo up until then.

But we had no idea that the ceiling vent which opened up so much in communication would eventually also open the door to a tragic hour of pain for all of us.

In all of these attempts to communicate in the Annex through 1968, the North Vietnamese were not simply playing the sleeping dog with us. There was constant harassment over the smallest things.

One day Bill Metzger was flush up against the peephole in the door trying to see out into the open courtyard. Bill's leg wound had healed over by now; it had taken six months to close up and had done so despite the lack of medical help from the Vietnamese. He had suffered his private hell in those six months. Not only had the wound continued to drain, but at night rats would come down the walls and gnaw on that wound or at his bedsores he'd gotten from lying in that bed for so long. It was not unusual on any night, about two in the morning, to wake up and hear him thrashing around, trying to get those rats out of his bed.

But now Bill had a raw scar where the wound had been, and he could get around by himself quite well. On this day, then, as he was peering out that peephole, he couldn't see through because of a large brown spot in the hole, so he backed up quickly to examine it. He realized with a shock that the "brown spot" was the eye of the guard we called Jawbone, and he came charging in, mad that Bill was trying to see out. He ordered Bill to kneel down. Bill refused. Jawbone kept insisting, so finally Bill got down, though it was hard on his leg, which was still very sore. Then Jawbone started slapping his face, and Bill kept staring back at him; the more he stared, the more Jawbone slapped him. After a half dozen or more licks, with Bill's face turning very red by then, Jawbone quit and left. But Bill never went up to that peephole again unless he was really sure no guards were around.

Twice I was taken out into the Quiz Room while in the Annex. There again Sweetpea grilled me about the workings of the communications system. Each time I went up I had to realize that I was dealing with dedicated people, dedicated to their own cause. The political types who did the questioning knew all the ways to probe and dig for answers.

So I'd sit there, and Sweetpea and the others would start with, "How are you? How is your family?"

I wouldn't look at them, so they forced me to. They always put me on a stool in front of them, always lower than they. Still I kept my eyes over their heads, never confronting their stares, because I could get mad easily, and I knew I couldn't win that way.

It would go on: "You have so many American troops in the South," Sweetpea said. "We have nobody in the South. You come to our country to invade, but we send no one to invade yours. . . ."

"But you do have soldiers in the South," I argued.

"Name one," he came back.

Of course, I could not. Silence. And I kept staring up above his head. He kept on hammering, trying to get me to renounce my government and becoming angry when I wouldn't; and the more I said, the more he would talk and hammer again, so it was best to sit there and take it. Everything in interrogations was shifting now to the political, away from communications and military information.

Now Sweetpea asked me again what I thought of the war, the U.S. involvement, if I didn't think it was a criminal act against North Vietnam. I knew, from what others had gone through, that they wanted a propaganda tape condemning the U.S. role.

At one point Sweetpea gave me a sheet of paper for me to write down my views. I wrote that, if I were President Johnson, I would escalate the war to end it. I referred to the Viet Cong as those who had to be stopped in their invasion of tne South, and what we were doing to stop them was right. I wrote about two pages, and when Sweetpea and the others read it they took issue with the use of "Viet Cong."

"It is properly the National Front of Liberation," Sweetpea snapped in that precise way. "You are forbidden to use that term again."

I sensed that was a face-saver—they did not want to be called Viet Cong, since identification with them was the wrong image.

They continued hammering at me, looking for weakness in me, wavering, something they could exploit. I decided right then to take a hard pro-U.S. line. The firmer the stand, I figured, the better off I would be. It was tough initially to take that stand, though, because I didn't want to be tortured again, and they kept threatening. The more they threatened, of course, the more difficult it was to hold to my views. But I had heard of prisoners who had softened up and died in torture as a result. Others I knew had cooperated fully and made the propaganda tapes. I didn't condemn them for that; I knew how hard it was to hold out—always the threat of those ropes, the beatings, the nights without sleep. Each man has a different threshold of pain, a different breaking point. I didn't know fully what mine was yet, and I was not anxious to find out. I decided, however, that if they knew I wouldn't give in easily to their political hammerings, that I wouldn't relent on my position on the United States' role in the war, they might pass me off.

For the moment, anyway, they did. They sent me back to my room while they read the rest of my statement. The next time around the keys jiggled in the lock in our room, my stomach knotted up, and I figured it was time again. Sure enough: back to the dingy, dimly lit room, the stool, the staring at the wall. But this time the approach was different. Sweetpea now asked me to make a tape for my family. I was eager for the opportunity to tell Dorothy I was okay. For all I knew, the Navy had listed me as Missing in Action, and not as a prisoner, which was one breath away from being listed as Killed in Action. The Navy knew I had ejected and landed in the jungle and had heard me say I was okay on the ground. But that was hardly enough to reassure her one way or the other.

So I said, "I would like to write to my family, but it would be wrong to make a tape, the wrong way to greet them." I knew if I made the tape they would play it over the *Voice of Vietnam*. I had heard such tapes over the compound P.A. that carried that station. It was great propaganda for them.

When I wouldn't make the tape, they let me go back to my room and took Tom Sterling out again. This time they told Tom he could write a letter to his wife, and I knew they were deliberately digging me for my failure to cooperate, trying to create resentment in me, bitterness toward Tom. To add salt to the wound, Sweetpea later came back with the letter Tom had written. He took great pains to show us the good stationery, the long form which Tom had been allowed to use. Then he let us feel the paper, look at the writing; finally he let Tom seal the letter while the rest of us watched longingly in silence, Tom looking a little embarrassed.

The next time Tom was called in to write a letter, we asked him to tell his wife to take pictures of the letter when she got it and have them developed. He did that. When

Sweetpea came back with that letter for us to feel, we had dipped our fingers in brick dust and left our prints all over the page. That way we figured Tom's wife, once having developed the film, could see the prints and maybe they could identify us in that way. We never did find out if that worked, but it gave us some satisfaction in knowing we had retaliated against Sweetpea, getting even a little.

Another time I asked Tom to tell his wife to make out a check for a gift to the Howard Memorial Fund, a scholarship fund my wife's parents had founded. I figured when my father-in-law got that check, he would know immediately that the only way Tom's wife could have gotten that information was from me. I never found out if that attempt worked, either.

It wasn't long, though, before Sweetpea and the others caught on to what we were doing. After a while anyone who was granted permission to write home had to do it in front of the interrogators.

I kept asking the camp commander about writing home, but he would say, "When your attitude improves, you will be able to write." It wasn't until the American people began to put pressure on the North Vietnamese about our treatment, to make a public issue of it, that the Vietnamese allowed us to write. That was later, in 1970. When that public pressure was felt, then the VC were demanding that we write home, and the shoe was on the other foot.

In the meantime we were being mentally tortured in this one area that was close to us, our families. Some men did make tapes to be sent to their wives. I was tempted to, of course, but I didn't and had some lively discussions with my roommates about this. They said I had too much pride about the thing. "So who cares if the tape gets on Radio Vietnam?" some would argue. "Nobody listens to it who matters. The main thing is your wife has the right to know about you." They were probably right, but I didn't regret holding out. It was, again, evidence of the will to resist, and I wanted to hang on to that.

Sometimes the interrogations with Sweetpea would become bizarre. He would get worked up and sometimes lose his composure.

"I want you to remember," he would yell at me, "that the ground in Vietnam is as deep as in the United States!"

I didn't know what that meant, but I supposed he was saying they didn't care one way or the other about my death. They would bury me in Vietnam if they had to.

Then he would go on, "You are in a Vietnam prison, not a U.S. hotel, do you understand?"

I would nod.

"Unless you repent of your war crimes, you will never go home—do you think you will go home?" The same old jab again.

"Yes, someday," I said.

"When, do you think?"

"We hope soon."

"No, it will not be soon. In fact, you will not go home until you are forty years old."

I had to smile inwardly at that, and I figured maybe the man's got something. Since forty was only five years away for me, pay dirt seemed in sight. For him, in his twenties, forty years of age was never.

I said, "No, the war can't go on that long."

My optimistic attitude triumphed again, as it kept doing in these hard days. But Sweetpea ended that line of conversation and went back to making the tape condemning U.S. involvement, which I said again I would not do.

As we went on day after day, we continued to keep the communications lines open, even though it cost us in the torture room. We devised unusual ways to do it too. Captain Jerry Denton even took to imitating the pigs the VC kept out back, and he would communicate in the same sound as the pigs, so that for a while we thought the pigs had learned the code.

Sometimes we would tell jokes through tapping under our door to the next room. When we learned to manage those nineteen-inch walls and get a signal through, we would tell jokes that way too. When a man liked the joke, he would tap rapidly on the wall. If he didn't like it, he would give slow, heavy thumps.

In order to make sure we didn't get trapped by the VC guards who were using our code to get the goods on us, we opened all of our communications with the familiar lyric "shave-and-a-haircut-two-bits." The VC, for some reason, could not figure out that rhythm in the code they knew we used, so by employing this as our signature anybody listening would know if it was a legitimate sender or a VC trying to pull a fast one.

We still got caught, though, and we often had to use our wits in a hurry. One day three men were at the wall of their room trying to communicate through those very thick concrete blocks. Another man was at the peephole at the door watching for any guards—unfortunately, he fell asleep standing up after long hours trying to communicate, and the guard came along, looked in, and saw the three men at the wall. It was WTG again, and he charged in, astounded that he actually had caught three men in the act.

Now confronted, the three men had to think fast to get out of it. One of them, who had had his blanket rolled up into a doughnut shape on the wall to talk into, simply said he was praying.

The second man, who had had his ear to the wall listening for an answer, said he was trying to hear if the food was on its way yet in the other room.

The third man, who had had his tin cup up against the wall to hear the code, said he had a mosquito inside and was listening to it die.

WTG simply stared at them, looked dumbfounded, and turned and walked out, shaking his head.

I was not an expert communicator myself, but when I did get word through I tried to be positive, to pass on good news or maybe a joke now and then.

I remember that once, before being shot down, I had visited Cubi Point in the Philippines. There was a shop there that made souvenir belt buckles that had the person's name inscribed on them. A lot of military men went in and bought these buckles and left them to be inscribed with their names on them. One man, Lieutenant Commander Duffy Hutton, was shot down before he could get back to pick up his buckle. I spotted it in the case in the shop. One day in the Zoo I heard that Duffy was in a certain building, so I swept down toward that room and tapped out the message for him, "Duffy, your belt buckle is ready at Cubi Point." Everybody got a laugh out of it, including Duffy. It was important that we laugh, to see the funny side, because everywhere we looked it was grim. The main purpose of this communication was to bolster one another's spirits as much as possible.

Later, in our insistence to communicate by every means, we were passing notes by floating them down a stream that ran through the camp. We called that stream the Charley James Memorial Canal, because a prisoner by that name was always cleaning it. Since the stream flowed downward, our communications naturally went always in that one direction; and someone got the idea that we could reverse the flow of the stream and float the notes upward. By pouring enough buckets of water from our well into that stream, we could in fact start moving it the other way. We tipped off the room next to us, and, sure enough, we got that stream to flow up—even though it confused Charley James considerably.

We passed notes through empty toothpaste tubes, in potatoes (when we got them), in bowls of rice, in anything that would move from room to room. Again, this let someone else know he was not alone.

Later in my imprisonment there was a young Navy flyer named Roger Lerseth whom we could hear screaming in the Quiz Room from the torture. By then he had a broken leg and both arms dislocated. He was in great pain. So we started singing songs to him loudly, and in those songs we asked him his name, his outfit, etc. It meant everything to Lerseth to hear American voices in that dark hour, telling him who we were, how we were organized, what to do, and so on.

I saw a lot of brave efforts on the part of prisoners in

their communications too. One man, Major Bob Purcell, a small man, maybe five feet ten, full of energy, shot down in 1965, took pains to learn the habits of the guards. He found out that they would check on him every twenty-five minutes, and, though he was living in solitary confinement, he managed in those off-periods to get up into that ceiling vent by himself and into the attic and to hurry along to the torture room with extra food, which he would drop through the vent to a man in torture. This took a lot of courage, because if he had been caught he would have been shot on the spot. Purcell would also hang out of his ceiling vent for as long as fifteen minutes, taking his chance on the guards, just to communicate to us. Later, when I was moved out to Camp Faith—a couple of years later, in fact—I looked up into the tree in my compound and there was Bob Purcell, making his rounds. I admired men like that who really took the initiative —at the risk of their lives.

Then there was J. J. Connell, who had been put in a kind of area camp where he had no contact with anybody else. His hands were useless. Part of that was actual injury, part of it was faked to escape torture. He pretended to have mental problems, so anything he told the VC would be considered too incredible to believe. He was a tough resister. He told the VC he was not married and had no children— when in fact he did—so when any packages came for him later he would not be given them. He had a remarkable memory. We could pass to him as many as twenty-eight to thirty messages a day by brooms, hand signals, and even coughs whenever we came anywhere near his building. And he would remember them all. In turn, he would pass this information on through notes he placed under his toilet bowl; when anyone came from the other buildings to pick up his bowl, they would get the word. The VC finally did not buy his playing at being mentally off, so they took him downtown for electric shock treatments in the hope of either jolting him out of his play-acting or else, if he was truly sick, getting his mind to snap back so he could tell them what they wanted to know. He had 120 days of that, so if he wasn't actually mentally disturbed before, he was by the time they finished with him. Meanwhile, when we began receiving packages from home later, in late 1969 and '70, we would send over to him a roll of mints or some other kind of candy, wrapped in plastic and delivered by pony express.

But later in 1970 J.J. just suddenly quit eating. And then he disappeared from the prison system. He was listed by the VC as having died, and I am sure that they did just let him die. He stands out, I think, as a symbol of the guts the American prisoners had in their long months and years of confinement.

All through this time—1967 and 1968—in the Annex, American bombing continued, always moving closer to our camp. We all viewed this bombing through our peepholes or through the vents in the ceiling. We would watch the flashes of the bombs and feel some elation. We couldn't fight the enemy here, but our guys were doing it for us. We had to grab onto all we could to keep our hopes alive.

But in March 1968 the bombing stopped, and the Paris peace talks began. I felt a new wave of optimism then. More and more people were beginning to ask me, "Red, when are we going home?"

I'd say, "Couple of months."

I kept saying this to them, because optimism was my forte. After a while other prisoners began to say about me, "Red is the guy who says the trucks didn't come to take us home this morning, but he says it could be this afternoon."

Sometimes a man would tap the word down from the farthest building and ask me for any straw of hope in the wind—and I would find one thing, anything, something, to prop him up and counter his pessimism.

Of course, nothing really came of my predictions, but it didn't matter. I still had hope that one day it would happen. It was hard at night, of course, to crawl back under my mosquito net and reflect on how hopeless the situation seemed. But I never allowed that thought to remain; I could not afford to.

And I would dream of home then, about the war ending,

returning to my family. Thinking about it would bring tears to my eyes. I didn't do much crying there, because it seemed a kind of self-pity to me. But there were times when I was close to the edge. On these nights when I thought about the possible ending of the war and visualized going home, I knew that our people in the States had to care about us. There was much antiwar activity going on then, and we heard about much of it over the Vietnam radio. Everybody wanted to quit and finish the U.S. involvement. We all wanted it finished too, but we hoped we wouldn't be forgotten in the pressure to wind it up. We also knew that the United States couldn't do much for us since its policy of dealing with this war could not be altered for a few hundred prisoners. Sometimes the feeling of being abandoned by people at home came on strong, but I had to believe—and I had to communicate my belief to the others—that it wouldn't go on forever, that there had to be an end to it, that we would not be forsaken, that we would come out alive, if we hung on.

And my thoughts would shift to my family. I was dreaming a lot lately about my children, what all this was doing to them, to my two happy-go-lucky boys and my precious baby daughter. I once saw Mike, my oldest boy, who was not more than nine then, in an accident. I woke up in a sweat. Then I thought of Dorothy and wondered how she was managing with no news, always having to wonder, never sure. I thought of the cruelty of that uncertainty for her. I prayed she would know I was alive, that God would give her that *feeling* if nothing else.

As I waited for sleep, with thoughts of home and Dorothy making me feel the acute pang of loneliness, I quoted the Twenty-third Psalm as I had been doing for many nights now, then the Beatitudes: "Blessed are the meek . . . blessed are the poor in spirit . . . blessed are the merciful . . ." And I wondered then why I had chosen those words to repeat; maybe it was because it was one passage I remembered from way back. No, as I thought over the words, I sensed the incongruity of them. I was asking for attributes that I knew could not win me anything with the North Vietnamese. I felt, then, that I was merely reciting the Scriptural passages to please God, to get Him more over on my side in hopes of getting better treatment, perhaps.

Could I say those words in front of WTG or Sweetpea or Jawbone? Would I dare? I felt uncertain in that moment, as if there were a part of the image of God I could not get into focus. So I went back to the Twenty-third Psalm and fought for sleep to put aside the nagging intuition that I was on a collision course of some kind with some awesome Truth that was about to be sprung on me.

6

The War Inside

DURING THE LONG NIGHT HOURS, through the endless months of captivity, I learned to pray, drawing on the goodness of God as my strength to face each new crack of light that meant another day. Praying gave me sleep, as well, the only time when I was completely free of the tension of captivity. But in the day, from first light on, I was forced to face the grittiness of clinging to the narrow edge of survival, to defend against the enemy that came in from several fronts. It wasn't only the Vietnamese guards and the ever-present threat of punishment or torture. As time wore on, we found that confinement with each other over such long periods of time brought its own test, sometimes pushing us to the breaking point.

For instance, one night, back in the Hanoi Hilton, Radio Hanoi had come on over the "box"—the P.A. in our room—telling the usual propaganda bits about American losses in the war. At one point they said America had lost more than four million men. Since there were hardly a total of three million in uniform in the entire services around the world, it was obviously absurd. It was even laughable.

Only I didn't laugh. It grated on me, even unnerved me. And that evening I took out my frustration on Metzger and Sterling, railing at them for not getting off their butts and communicating more. That was the first time I had lost my cool with anybody, and there was a long, heavy silence following it. We went to bed, finding some kind of withdrawal under our mosquito nets. Some time in the night I got up to urinate and missed the toilet bowl, going down my leg instead. Both Sterling and Metzger saw and heard that and began to laugh in the dark, smothering it as best they could so I wouldn't hear. I ignored them and went back to bed even madder.

When morning came, though, I sensed how funny that really was, and I apologized to both of them for blowing up. I had to thank God for the humorous things that saved the mounting tension that would come between us in those small rooms. For, while we had to face the pressure of torture every day from the outside—the battle against boredom, depression, anxiety, and the problem of just plain living together—that had its effect as well.

After months of being cooped up with the same roommates even in the larger rooms, I became conscious of the irritating habits some had, even as they surely were conscious of mine. Just the way a man burped would get on my nerves—the way a man walked, the peculiarities of his movements, the same hitch in his stride, began to play on me and I would think, "Why can't he walk differently now and then?" After a while the conversation with the same roommates would become repetitious, but, when a roommate began to repeat the same stories back to me that I had given him with a few additional imaginative frills, I again realized we'd been together too long.

Some men wanted to sleep late in the morning, some wanted to get up early to exercise. Some men had the habit of getting up at night and urinating dead center into the toilet bowl in a loud musical sound that woke me up. Others hit the side of the bowl—and some didn't hit it at all.

One prisoner we had with us briefly always had his eyes closed in prayer. He stayed like that in his corner or on his bed, which was an attempt to withdraw from the sordidness of the environment. When he did open his eyes, he took one look around, saw that nothing had changed, and promptly locked his eyes shut again. I sympathized with him at first, then became impatient with him for withdrawing like that when everybody's energies were needed to work for all.

The only way I could cope with these little things was to try to ignore them. In a like situation at home I could always get away from the irritating habits or remarks of others, get some reprieve. But in a nine-by-twelve, locked in, there was no place to go. I was stuck with them from daybreak to dark, as were they with me. The only way to keep those irritations from exploding was to force myself not to let it get to me, and this was often a matter of pure will.

One man in my room, who had a bad case of saying depressing things, always said in the darkness as he settled down to sleep under his mosquito net, "Infinity minus one." It was a bad commentary for all of us trying to stay on top of things and remain optimistic.

Sometimes I would be looking out my peephole in the door and see another American prisoner outside from another room. I would call another of my roommates over to take a look and see if he recognized him. Well, in the interim, the man moved and another American came into view. So when I described the man I had seen to the roommate who was seeing another, we both began to claw at each other about the description of the man. This would go on and on, until one of us got some sense and broke it off.

Food was always a constant source of tension and frustration. Sometimes the Vietnamese would give an extra ration to somebody in our room who seemed sickly, at least to them. They could not stand to see a prisoner going down like that, so they fed him extra portions as a face-saving gesture. But who would get it was their decision and not ours. Often, therefore, the food designated for a prisoner who "looked poorly" was not justified. There would be someone else who needed it more. This would create a lot of tension with the others in the room. I saw men lowered to animals in stealing food for themselves, because the first law of preservation was to eat. Some men would always be first to get the hot soup that came, denying others in the room who were sick and needed it more. Sometimes this kind of tension would bring a blowup, and I would hear scuffling in another room around mealtime and know a fistfight had broken out.

And yet there were others who, even though they were down in weight maybe sixty to seventy pounds, would take the food off their plates and give it to someone else they felt was worse off. Captain Jerry Denton stands out in my mind as one of those heroes, always shortchanging himself in his own ration to give it to someone else. Some of the prisoners bowed to the pressure of survival with the food, but many others would not lower themselves. Even so, it wasn't until we organized our rooms according to rank and imposed discipline in the food that we were to avoid serious breakdowns. I had to admit that there were times when I wanted to haul off on someone who kept thinking only of himself.

Sometimes the poor rations drove us to extreme ends to satisfy our hunger. One day Metzger and Austin were watching a furry caterpillar crawling up the wall. Metzger finally plucked it off, turned to me, and asked, "How about a bite, Red?" I thought he was kidding. When I laughed, Metzger promptly bit into the caterpillar, then gave some to Austin. They ate the creature with no ill effects. It pointed out the extremity of our needs, so it was not surprising that we had problems with food.

Later on we began to get word that there were antiwar delegations coming to Hanoi for visits, and some of their statements came over the "box." We had hoped that maybe these visits from American dignitaries would help our cause —get us better treatment, at least. But as we listened to their statements, condemning the war and the U.S. role in it, we realized that we were being tortured to get us to say the very things being said by our own people right here in Hanoi. We tried to put all of it in a proper context, to appreciate what was being attempted by these well-meaning people; but locked in as we were, half starving to death, with no hope of ever being released, facing torture all the time, it began to grate on us. There seemed to be a new pall of despair hanging over us, and there was a lot more bitching in the rooms. "So what the hell's the use?" was the common response. And this would spread through the room, and it took all I had as the "positive rumormonger" to get the good word back in focus, back into our thinking.

These statements crushed some prisoners completely, and they never got back up—as we called it, they "let their balloon go." As for myself, I simply had to find a way to allow for such things, as hard as they seemed at the moment. I knew the war in Vietnam had caused a lot of debate, with high feelings on both sides at home. Being locked in prison for our part in it as military men was one side, too, and it was all we could see at the moment. We just had to accept the fact that there was that other side—so all I could do was allow for that and try to keep my mind on other things. The North Vietnamese, of course, used every statement, projected every film they could about the antiwar business at home. But we simply had to face the reality of the antiwar movement and defend against it as best we could, because to allow ourselves to be put down by it was only one more means to break us.

And, of course, what built further tension and frustration was that the Vietnamese were always offering a way out just by cooperating with them, by making a tape or coming through with a confession they could use. A man could seriously believe it—that he would get a better deal, the needed medical treatment, better food, etc. There were two men, as a case in point, who did cooperate with the VC by making a book of cartoons condemning the U.S. involvement in the war and playing up the "humane and compassionate treatment" of the Vietnamese in the prison. One cartoon showed a downed American flyer being welcomed by the North Vietnamese to a prison cell with all the comforts of home—radio, nice bed, good food. This was an unfortunate thing to do, but they did it in hopes of getting an early release from the prison, since there were rumors that some people might be allowed to go home.

The book of cartoons landed in our room when Rabbit

insisted that Major Al Runyan, senior man in our cell, should draw in the borders for the book, give it that final artistic flourish. That was the VC method—make someone cooperate in a project condemning the United States and then force someone else who would not normally do so to be a part of it. Al complained of bad eyes, and in fact he was having trouble, so they hauled him off to the Quiz Room. After a few days of pressure, Rabbit came in with a pair of glasses and said, "These glasses are for people between forty and forty-five years of age. So use them and get busy."

After a lot of pressure, Al finally consented to paint in those borders with a charcoal pen; it was frustrating to him to be a part of it, and it made us all angry that Al was put in such a position. And the two cartoonists never did get released as the VC promised; for all their nonresistance to the VC and cooperation, they landed right back in the prison compound anyway and wound up in our building in the Hilton. Having them in with us, knowing what they had done, made it a bit tense at first, but after a while, realizing they had been taken, they began cooperating with us in our plan of resistance.

The point was, however, that other men saw that some were cooperating with the VC, some were going downtown to make tapes—and for all they knew, these people were getting a better deal. Some, in fact, were (even though the two cartoonists hadn't fared so well). Every day, then, the mind had to play with that possibility, of maybe giving in a little in hopes of getting something back, a better food ration, perhaps, or maybe some badly needed medical help.

But it was the guards who gave us the most frustration. To beat a guard at his game of harassment was the high point of any day. One thing we hated in 1967 and 1968 during the bombing raids was the fact that we had a fox-hole dug in our rooms for protection. And every raid found us having to climb down into that clammy six-by-six hole shaped like a grave. During the rainy season the bottom of that hole would fill with water, and there was nothing worse than to sit in that or have your feet sunk into it for the hours that raids were on. After the 1968 halt to the bombing, the guards finally told us to fill in that foxhole, which we did. One of the men in the room, however, came up with an idea —once the hole was filled, he put a makeshift wooden cross on it. When the guard, WTG, came in to check on the room, he looked at the cross and appeared puzzled. He thought a moment, then he looked at me and said, "No good. Take out." I said no. He repeated his demand. Still I refused, so he stormed out. While he was gone, the man who had made the cross dug a trench under the cross and attached a string to the base of it and covered it with dirt again. Again, WTG came in, looked at the cross, and demanded we take it out. We refused. So he promptly went over to it to give it a kick. Well, just as he lifted his foot, my roommate who was holding the string gave it a jerk. The cross moved. The guard paused with his foot still in the air, staring down at the cross, and then, without another word, did an about-face and tore out of the room in a cloud. We never heard from that guard again.

There was the time another guard, who was new, decided he would fulfill his daily quota of harassments. One day we watched him as he paused in front of one of the rooms down the line: He would hitch up his pants; put an awful scowl on his face to look mean; and then go up to the door, throw the bolt with a loud, resounding clatter, throw the door open so that it hit the wall and then shout into the room, "Queekly! Bowl!" And the shock of all that kind of hit the room with a blitz, but they immediately got their toilet bowl and emptied it.

The guard went to the other rooms doing the same thing, until he came to the room next to ours. Once again he hitched up his pants, put on the scowl, hit the bolt, slammed the door open and yelled, "Queekly! Bowl!" Well, because he was new, he didn't know that room was empty, and he stood there a long ten seconds staring into the emptiness, trying to recover. But instead of closing the door and coming on to my room, he turned and left—in order to save face. He couldn't go on with the ceremony knowing we knew the room was empty. We took great delight in this, and when we couldn't engineer a way to make the guards lose face, sometimes the Lord smiled on us and devised His own way. Of that I am sure.

What used to annoy us greatly at times was the way the guards would parrot our American slang. One guard, Little Caesar, used to say, "You must keep your nose clean and walk the straight and narrow or you will be here 'til the cows come home!"

Or the guard we called The Creep or Pox, because he had pock marks all over his face, tried to pick up one of our slang expressions: "Screw you!" He tried it on me one day and it came out, "Why you screw you me?" Yet, for all the savageness he sometimes showed us, he would also see to it we had extra food, and we could never figure that out. But we could never count on his consistency in providing extra rations, for sometimes, instead of extra food, he would hit us across the face with his shoe. This kind of treatment kept us constantly on our toes in fear.

One day Rabbit said to me, "I have dug holes all over Vietnam and never found hell." I didn't know what he meant, or what he was trying to get out of me. So I didn't know whether to answer him, engage him in conversation, or keep silent. To talk to him about hell and heaven might get me another slap from his rubber sandal.

To counter their frequent boasts about their supreme powers and advancement, one of the prisoners coined a maxim just to get back at them: "The Vietnamese civilization is four thousand years behind civilization and catching up by working one day a month." We never said that to them directly because it would merit reprisals, but finding such ways to offset them was the means to cut down our frustration in their harassment of us.

Medical problems continued to build the frustration. Our teeth were going bad, and dentistry in North Vietnam is primitive at best. We did not get a dentist until 1971. I had an abscessed molar by then, very painful, and the North Vietnamese dentist went at extracting it without Novocain—

they didn't have it. His "attack" was not good in the first place, and the pulling was a dragged-out process, while my whole head seemed to be ready to explode from the pain. It was the worst ordeal I had, apart from torture.

Until the dentist showed up, we improvised by taking tobacco out of our cigarettes and packing it into our aching cavities; the nicotine seemed to help. Men who had ear infections and couldn't get the VC to understand—if the VC could not see the illness, they would do nothing—would urinate into their tin cups and pour the urine into their ears to help cut the infection. I don't know that it helped, but it was probably the act of *trying something* that did more than the possible remedy. Later, one of the men received some Terramycin in a package; but even these pills didn't help our ear problems, so we pulverized them and blew the powder into each other's ears. This seemed to do the job, although it was rather messy.

One night I heard one of the men continually trying to clear his throat during sleep. Hack. Hack. Hack. To our astonishment, when we checked him, it was a tapeworm trying to get up through his throat passages. The worm problem was common in Vietnam, and some men would chew tobacco and swallow it trying to clear them, because I had said we used to give our horses at home that remedy for their worms; for the men, however, it didn't seem to help much. The worms were a constant irritant. Sometimes these worms would crawl out their rectums, and it was not unusual to see one of the few Vietnamese children on the compound passing a twelve-inch worm. Since it was something the Vietnamese accepted as a part of their lives, it was impossible to convince them we needed medicine for it.

We were also plagued with whipworms, which would irritate us constantly. At night when we were sleeping, the muscles in our anus relaxed, these whipworms would crawl out of our rectums, because they had to come out to lay their eggs. There is no more uncomfortable feeling to wake up to than that.

Dysentery was a constant companion. Rats and dirty

water accounted for most of it—and since at least a half a pound of dirt came in the average soup bowl, dysentery was not surprising. Diarrhea weakened a lot of prisoners, and the VC would give medicine for it, but it depended on how many times a man had to use the toilet bowl. Pain did not mean a thing to the VC. One prisoner used the toilet seventy-two times in a week and finally got some medicine; it didn't help much, however. Flies were the main carriers of dysentery, and they were everywhere. Someone called the blue-tailed fly the North Vietnamese national bird.

In 1970 we were sent medicine in our packages from home. But the North Vietnamese only once allowed us to receive that medicine; the rest of the time they kept it for themselves. When the expiration date on the medicine passed, they came to our rooms and destroyed the medicine in front of us. It was just one more way they had of turning the screw.

Meanwhile, the rats continued to plague us. They were, of course, the number one health hazard. At one time, when the lights were out due to a heavy bombing raid, the rats came up into our rooms at night and ran over us as we slept. These were the kind that could run straight up flat walls with no problem. At one time they took to digging holes under our rooms and creating a fuss, so, when we got some concrete from the VC to patch up our courtyard wall, we sealed these holes. We listened to those rats desperately trying to get out, and we got some satisfaction in defeating this lesser enemy anyway. But the stench of those dead rats under our rooms was to linger for weeks.

The rats were bad enough as a health hazard, but we also had the problem of backed-up sewers later on. Every time they backed up, we would have to go out, climb down into that muck, and unplug them, and we smelled for days—until we were allowed to wash it off.

Then there was the cigarette problem. We were issued three cigarettes a day to begin with, and the ration increased as we went along. I had quit smoking back home, but now I was taking my share and smoking—to get anything at all from the guards was a major breakthrough. And, besides, smoking was an event, something to do, something to break up the pattern of monotony; we looked forward to it. But, though we received the cigarettes, we did not get matches, so we had to wait until a guard came around to light us up. Sometimes he would come before a meal, sometimes shortly after a meal, sometimes later still. We would sit waiting and asking: Is he going to come? Has he forgotten? What has happened? Sometimes the cigarette ration was cut, and we were back to one cigarette, or sometimes none, and the question then was: Will we get any today?

Sometimes prisoners who were hooked on cigarettes would move around after dark looking for the leftover butts and stick them in their kits to smoke later. We called these men the "silent butlers."

One guard, The Slug, whom I was to get to know only too well later on, occasionally stole our ration of cigarettes. We had three men in the room, each to get three cigarettes —but one did not smoke. Instead of giving us that extra ration, Slug would steal those cigarettes for himself. Finally one of the men in the room got tired of losing out to Slug, so one day he took the tobacco out of three of his own and replaced it with human feces. He left them out for Slug to see and, he hoped, lift. Slug never stole our cigarettes after that.

We finally managed to beat the no-match business, too, by making a punk of toilet paper and lighting it from our cigarettes. We kept it burning in the room as long as we could—or as long as the guards did not catch on, since they would forbid this if they found out. It was part of their demand for control of every facet of our lives, designed to bring our nerves up to the edge of sanity.

The cigarette supply became a part of the medical treatment after a while. A lot of the men, strangely enough, were beginning to get asthma attacks, for no reason, and we couldn't figure it out. The attacks occurred in winter when the northeasterly wind blew. Somehow the guards were convinced that smoking helped asthma, and they allowed the asthma cases to have matches occasionally. Again, such illness bothered the Vietnamese, who felt it was a bad commentary on their "humane treatment" of prisoners. There were about fifteen to twenty people affected with this asthma, and it was pathetic to see them laboring, shaking, with every breath. Some of them took to smoking, believing, as the Vietnamese did, that it helped them to breathe; but I doubted it. So we would wake up some nights with a man dragging for breath, and we would yell, *"Bao cao!"* calling for a guard to bring medicine. They seldom responded, and some of our men wanted to storm the walls because of it; seeing their comrades sick and helpless was too much. Sometimes the whole room would yell in unison, *"Bao cao!"* and only then did the guards come and give the patient an adrenalin shot.

Some of these asthma cases had to sit up all night to try to sleep. Some went three to four months sitting up that way; some almost died from the attacks. Nobody knew what caused this, because the afflicted men never had had allergy problems before as far as they knew.

We had one officer, twenty-six years old, who had a severe case of asthma and insisted that smoking helped it. He was smoking up to sixteen cigarettes a day, taking rations from those who didn't smoke, and he insisted it helped him breathe better. I finally decided he had to quit to save his lungs, and I told him that, if he would quit, I would quit, starting the next day. But he was moved out that night, so we didn't get started. Maybe it was better for us that he was moved out, because sometimes the other men would vent their frustrations on a sick man, since the leaders in the room gave him preferential treatment with medicine and food.

We had another prisoner, Dave Rehmann, who had a badly deformed arm from an injury after shoot-down. It had been broken and set and then became disjointed and grotesque. That arm was to drain for four or five years. One day he saw a little string sticking out of the arm and pulled on it. Out came a long cord, about an eighth of an inch in diameter, which had been left inside when they operated.

Some men suffered more frustrations than others. Major Dwight Sullivan, a fine man, never received any packages from home when we were finally allowed packages in late 1969. He was flying an F-105 and collided with a wingman and had to bail out. The crew of the other two planes in the collision got out and were seen parachuting down, but no one saw Sullivan's chute. His family figured he had been lost. I used to watch Sullivan, because I lived with him for a year, and the demoralizing effect of not receiving packages when all the rest did hit him very hard. He took it without complaining, and I admired him for that; but whenever the packages were finally all distributed he would ask, "Do you think there will be more?" We all kept hoping Sullivan would get one, and after a while I wanted him to have mine, because it seemed so cruel for one man to be denied all the time. All we could do was share with him from ours, but it wasn't the same as getting his own. For three years Sullivan went on like that, watching everyone else get a package, always hoping—but losing hope too. Then one day, when I went up to get my package, I saw his name on a package, his wife's name on the return. I raced back to the room to tell him, and there is no way to express the light on that familiar face, which had been in shadow so long. After three years of waiting, of being presumed dead, with no word, nothing, now he had it, the thing that mattered, that was so intimate, that had so much feeling of love in it. But all I could think of as Sullivan fondled that package was the years of tension that had torn at him—the frustration, the loneliness, the emptiness that almost destroyed him.

Even trying to get a shave could create problems. In the early days in 1967 we shaved once a week, all using the same razor. The blade became dull and worn out, of course, and this made it even more difficult. Later we got to shave twice a week, then every third day. We had to dry-shave, since there was no lather. Then they took the mirrors away from us for a two-year period, so we had to shave each other. Sometimes we used our cup and put a little water in the bottom to get a reflection; sometimes we put water on the floor in the same attempt. We tried to get the mirrors back, but the VC had caught some of our men using them to signal with, so we could not have them. This was a blessing in disguise, really, because we could not see our gaunt, haggard faces.

Some of the men grew beards, but the lice gathered in a hurry. It seemed this was going to create one more health problem, so we forbade it. Sometimes men would grow a beard as a protest—the VC didn't like beards either—and then proceed to use it as a point of trade: They would shave if the VC would let them write home. I don't know if it worked too well, but it was worth a try.

The guards had other peculiar rules that irritated us to no end. One was that we couldn't wash with our clothes off. We always had to wear a pair of trousers. Some of the men complained bitterly about this; they deliberately stripped down in front of the guards and created real problems for the room leaders. Later, the guards finally built partitions for us to get behind when we stripped down; but it took several months to get that concession, and in the meantime there were a lot of short tempers.

Of all of these frustrations with the routine and regulations, it was, perhaps, the long Sunday afternoons or the hours after four every day that got to us the most—those hours when time hung heavy and we hunted for things to do. When I was in the Hanoi Hilton, after my shoot-down I had made a small ball from the leavings of Metzger's bandages; and every day in that long, empty time block, I would throw that thing up to the ceiling and catch it with my good hand. My left hand was still useless from that first torture in the Hilton right after shoot-down, the nerves having been damaged. It would take a good six months to regain use of the hand. So there I would lie, throwing that ball of bandages up into the air . . . up and down . . . up and down . . . I counted five thousand catches within a few days as I tried to make this pastime fill the void that would keep me from losing my sanity in those endless hours of nothing to do but think and wonder.

Then in the long hours of the evening, American ingenuity had to take over. Fortunately it did. Some nights when I was living with Dwight Sullivan, who was a baseball fan, we would go over all the big plays in the past World Series games. Before getting in with Sullivan, I had tried to reconstruct the 1950 Philadelphia Phillies Whiz Kid team and had come up with all the positions except the second baseman. Then Sullivan gave me that.

On other nights we would get together as a group, rather than retreat to our beds and mosquito nets, and one man would host the rest of the room for the evening. We would fantasize going to his house, and there he would serve hors d'oeuvres, then the meal—a menu we would all lovingly concoct in our imaginations.

Sometimes Bill Austin or Jack Van Loan would tell stories long into the night—Hemingway, Faulkner, others. And they were such good storytellers, putting emotion into the lines, that we found the hours would slip by. *Gone with the Wind, Advise and Consent, The Caine Mutiny*—all of them came to life for us under the narrative talents of both these men.

Sometimes we would take an imaginary trip in the early evening, and we would go to a city one of us had visited. Sometimes we would take our wives out, and we would go through the entire evening in our imagination—what we ate, what we did for entertainment. We learned a lot of geography then, and after a while we began to call on men in the groups who had knowledge in various fields that they could share with us, even teach us. This was the nucleus of a series of special class lectures in a larger set of over fifty-five such class hours taught later on in Camp Faith ten miles north. Everything from botany to cooking to family counseling, to mathematics and the Bible.

We made every effort and activity count in "using" time:

We washed our clothes for a longer period, just to stay busy; we stretched our meals out longer.

Some nights I would retreat inside my mosquito net and count the holes in it, from right to left, up and down. I remember counting ninety-eight little squares from one end to the other on one side; each square had four hundred tiny holes. The top from left to right—the small side—had thirty-eight squares. Down the sides, forty-two squares. The holes in all these squares ran into the millions.

Sometimes I would lie there thinking about money, and I would visualize my wife saving what she could of mine and what we would do with it when I returned. But the pleasure I derived from this activity began to fade with the accumulation of months and years in the prison; monetary values did not count in this environment. I began to take inventory of myself, and the spiritual became the prominent vein of thought. Others were beginning to feel the same, so we formed a Daily Prayer Club, which was responsible for coming up with one spiritual thought a day. I began to quote Bible verses I had memorized from my childhood and church, some verbatim but many paraphrased. Others began to do the same. I wish I had memorized more in my early years.

Later, when we got a copy of the Bible during a time of good treatment, we immediately set out to get as much of it copied down as we could. First we took down the whole Gospel of Matthew, because it had the favorites such as the Sermon on the Mount and the Christmas story. And once we had it on paper, Ralph Gaither, who had a terrific photographic mind, memorized it all just in case we never got a copy of the Bible again.

With that Bible, I took to learning a lot of Scripture myself. Even the agnostics and atheists wanted to read that Bible—some, of course, only to argue the points about the existence of God—but many of them to grab onto something that could give hope. If one person was copying it, someone else might get mad because it was not available to read.

But to copy it meant we would have it for all to use. We finally had to post a reading list for the Bible, each man taking a certain time; some men had to get up at three A.M. to get their turn, but they never missed.

I began early, in my time in the Annex, to lead the prayer before every meal, and the others in my cell accepted this. One prayer I often used, because it seemed relevant to the situation, was that adopted by the Alcoholics Anonymous group: "GOD, GRANT ME THE SERENITY TO ACCEPT THE THINGS I CANNOT CHANGE, THE COURAGE TO CHANGE THE THINGS I CAN, AND THE WISDOM TO KNOW THE DIFFERENCE."

We began to appreciate the "small" things that would offset our frustration at what we considered the big things. Once Jim Clement's mother sent him a bottle of Pub shaving lotion, and the highlight of the week would be on Saturday night when we got to shave. We would use a little smidgen of that Pub and the smell of it hung on for days, countering the musty odors of the drab rooms we were in.

Some of the men were lucky to get Dial soap in their packages and shared it with us in the showers; it was a nice-smelling soap. Some had enough to use every other day. When they would pass our room, even a hundred yards away, we could smell that soap, and it gave us a lift and helped us to face up to the irritations that, though sometimes small, grew to be very big in that tense atmosphere.

We even devised equipment for games, like chess, checkers, Acey Deucey. We made poker chips out of bread, colored some red with brick dust, others black with cigarette ashes. I never got into the poker games, though; since I knew how much hard feeling came from running up an endless pot of money in these games, we limited the games to $500, no more. Having done that, however, I did not feel I could then enter into the game, having helped set those limits.

We even played duplicate bridge. Most people would pair off, and consequently it became very competitive. We needed that competition. We didn't have much reason to strive for anything here, and winning was everything. It was the same way going up to torture, we told ourselves; it was a game. The Vietnamese on one side, we on the other. Winning for us was refusing to give them anything they wanted; winning for them was to break a man so that he cooperated in making the tapes or in giving information. With that kind of philosophy, we could manufacture something to look forward to, and in our games we would plan our strategy, think out every move, fight to come out on top. Ken Fleenor and I, who were both bad losers, fought out a chess game for a whole week, but it kept us going, filling in the long hours, giving us that reprieve from the tensions of living together.

So all we could do was to meet the frustrations within us head on, and it called for willingness to work at it, for ingenuity in order to beat it. I was proud of every effort and of every man who gave it. We faced up to our long empty hours together, and our ingenuity led to an amazing program of teaching that was to give every man hope in those hours and that was to develop later on into "Hanoi University."

In all of this, we continued to communicate. When the VC put us out in the gardens to work, sometimes this garden would be behind a building we had not been able to communicate with, so we pounded out the code in the clumps of dirt with our shovels. The VC, of course, were not shrewd enough to catch on. Another tack was the following: When a guard was next to me, I would look at him and direct a question at him in English, a question a guy in the building could hear. The guard, either B. O. Plenty or WTG, would look at me queerly, not comprehending—and not realizing that I was communicating with the man inside.

We pounded out the code on our walls, taking polls as to the most beautiful movie star—I voted for Rhonda Fleming, but Liz Taylor won. The athlete of the century turned out to be Jim Thorpe, though I voted for Joe Di Maggio. The man of the century was Winston Churchill, far and away. The poll showed Adolf Hitler to be the one who had made the biggest impact on history in the twentieth century. And so we entertained ourselves as best we could.

When I got my orders in May 1968 to move over to the

Zoo, which was directly behind my present location, I had no idea what was about to happen. By then I had become a pretty good communicator. I had made my optimism work for a number of men. My faith was becoming sharper as I reevaluated my spiritual life. I was beginning to feel this thing could be whipped. The way the camps were joining together into the communications link, we were now becoming a unit, resisting together, learning to live together.

But all of that was to go on the line in the memorable months ahead. I thank God He did not let me see it coming.

7

Escape and My Darkest Hour

THERE WERE NIGHTS in the Annex when Bill Austin and I talked about escape. Sometimes it was not serious talk, but something merely to occupy our minds. We knew about the code of conduct according to which it was the prisoner's responsibility to escape when possible, but even beyond this the urge to make it out to freedom was often overpowering.

There had been an escape attempt in October 1967 when Air Force Captain George McKnight and Navy Lieutenant (jg) George Coker managed to get out. They floated down the Red River for about fifteen miles until they got chilled and decided to come out and try to go it on land. They were picked up immediately by Vietnamese civilians. The VC did not punish them, because both men said the attempt was out of desperation—they felt they would die in prison anyway so they might as well try it. After that, however, the camps were on very tight security. Later, in December 1969, there was yet another attempt—this one by Colonel Ben Purcell—but he did not get very far before being picked up. He was put in a punishment camp called Skid Row, because it was twice as bad as anything in the "normal" prison environment, reserved for those who were incorrigible.

As Austin and I talked about it in the Annex in late 1968,

we weren't sure it was possible to make a successful break-out and make our way the hundreds of miles to the sea or to friendlies in the south. For one thing, Hanoi sat on the Red River Delta, where several hundred thousand people lived. Even if we did make it out of the compound, the people in Hanoi were dedicated to tracking down any foreigners and were promised $1,500 by the government for every American flyer they caught. It would be tough trying to get through that kind of "police force." What's more, the average North Vietnamese is about five feet two inches tall, with black hair, yellow-skinned, slant-eyed. How would I, at six feet three inches, now about 160 pounds, with red hair, fair-skinned, and round-eyed, fit into that population if I tried to use its traffic patterns to get to the sea?

And there was another problem, that of environment— the miles of jungle, the thick, cruel bush that a man would have to negotiate to get out. To illustrate the nature of the land we were living in, Bill Austin killed a poisonous snake in our room one night, and in the morning when we emptied our toilet bowls, we hung it up on the fence. We watched that snake periodically through the door peephole, and in three hours it had been completely devoured by insects. Nothing was left of it—nothing. We knew the same thing could happen to us if we tried to make it 110 miles to the sea.

For all that, we still spent time thinking up ways to break out of the prison itself. Austin and I managed, after weeks of labor, to get the inner metal doors off their hinges. It really would have been no problem to walk straight out the door if we wanted to. And then one night in the room next to us, where Captain Konrad Trautman and three others lived, the guard had forgotten to lock the door altogether. That was a rare occasion, but it happened, and the men there thought all night of that unlocked door. In the morning Trautman pounded out the message to us that the door had been open all night and then added, "But where to next?"

That about summed it up. If we did get out, where to

then? There were too many obstacles to success. And, unless we had help from the outside, someone coming in with the means to jump us out of there completely, it would be suicide to try it.

Well, in May 1968, I was moved again—this time to the Zoo, which was directly behind the Annex. We had not known it was there until earlier that year, when Major Al Runyan came into the Annex from the Zoo. I moved over to a building in the Zoo called the Garage with Runyan and Ken Fleenor. The layout of this camp was the same as the Annex, except there were eight buildings instead of five.

The Garage was directly behind the fifteen-foot wall separating the Zoo from the Annex, and, since we knew the layout of the Annex, we began to set up a communications system that would link the Zoo and the Annex, which up to now had not been established. I reasoned that, if we could bring the 118 men in the Zoo into contact with the 72 men in the Annex, we would have much more going for us.

The only way to get through that fifteen-foot wall that separated the two compounds, then, was to toss notes over the top or try to communicate through the ceiling vents of our rooms. We ran our "pony express" in the same way, but could not cross over to the Annex with that wall between us. Still, we managed to make our communication work very well.

Meanwhile, the Paris Peace Talks had resulted in our getting our first food packages from home; they arrived in February 1969. A few good things were happening about then in the prison. More of our wounded people were being taken to the hospital. Too, we were getting a little more food, and better food too—sometimes bread with our soup now, sometimes some canned meat, sometimes candy. The VC, however, were demanding that we make tapes telling of the "good" treatment. This most of us never did.

During the early spring of 1969, unknown to me, a nine-man committee which included Major John Dramesi and Major Ed Atterbury was storing extra food rations the Vietnamese were giving us—the result again of pressure in the Paris Peace Talks—hiding them up in the attics of their rooms. There were, of course, sick people who would not eat, and these men used their rations to put into an emergency kit for a breakout.

I was to remember that night of May 10, 1969, when John Dramesi and Ed Atterbury broke out. They climbed out of Room 6 in the Annex, up through the ceiling vent, down the wall, across the compound, and over the wall near the Quiz Room. I didn't know it until the message was pounded out to the entire complex, and I sensed then that we were going to be in for it.

Sure enough. For three weeks the Vietnamese, in a kind of rage, took out twenty men to the torture room. Others were given the psychological approach and offered a deal: If they would talk and tell who was responsible for the escape, they would receive benefits in return. A lot of people lied under the torture, telling the Vietnamese anything to get relief, and each man was forced to put his finger on someone else. They couldn't be blamed, for the news went around that Atterbury had been caught and had died in the torture, so everybody knew this was a serious matter, and a man had to look out for himself. Dramesi, too, was recaptured. I knew it was only a question of time before they put the finger on me, because I was right in the center of the communications system.

On the night of June 14, 1969, they came for us. I heard the key in the lock, and my stomach jumped as it always did at that sound. Somehow I knew this was going to be the big one—that what I had up to now was kid stuff. They took Al Runyan out first, because he was the senior man in the room; then they came for Major Ken Fleenor. Finally they came and got me. I was told to take my drinking cup and suit up. The guard's bayonet prodded me along past the two rooms where Al and Ken had been taken, until we reached the last room in the building called the Chicken Coop.

I looked around the room. It had not been swept, and it was very dusty. It was lighted by a fifteen-watt bulb, which dangled from the ceiling like a piece of rotten fruit left behind in a tree. The switch to it was simply two wires hooked together. The door to the room had a blue curtain hanging over it, and the bottom was draped to about six inches from the floor. The windows had glass—the only glass in Vietnam, I supposed—but that didn't help, because boards were nailed over the glass, so there was no light coming in.

Now I sat there in that room, which was like a coffin; they put leg irons on me like loop-shaped U-bolts, with the large leg iron in between serving as the eyes of the U-bolts intertwining both ankles, which was to make sure I did not escape.

I started yelling *"Bao cao!"* right away; I wanted an interpreter so I could ask why I was being put into irons, since the escape was not from my building. But they ignored it. They continued putting on the irons and I kept yelling *"Bao cao!"*—again to no avail. Then my arms were locked behind my back with wrist irons, very tight. They were turning it on this time, rougher than they'd ever been. Somehow I sensed that this was the point I had been heading for all along; this was the crucial test to my own faith, to the sense of optimism I had tried to maintain all these months. Now it was going to be a battle between them and me; one of us was going to come out of this on top, and there seemed little hope that I could, that I would ever live through it. Yet I knew I had to try, to use all I had within me to resist.

Finally an officer came in, and I recognized The Rat—not Sweetpea this time, as I had expected. I knew for sure, then, that the interrogation was going to get serious. I looked up at his sharply defined features, long hair, pointed nose, dark-skinned face, and that belt wrapped around his middle; he had on rubber tire sandals. Joining him was Hanoi Fats, who had the extra thirty pounds to use to throw us around if we needed it. There was one other guard, fairly new to me, whom we called Switches, a man with a hating look. He would put the torture on when it was time, of that I was sure.

The Rat began with, "What building do you live in?"

"I don't know the name," I said. "It doesn't have a name."

"Who is the senior ranking officer in the camp?"

"I don't know."

He unloosed the irons that held my hands behind my back and made me drop my pants onto the floor, and I got down spread-eagled under his command, with my bare buttocks exposed. Then Switches took a rubber fan belt about three and a half feet long, an inch in diameter, which had a knot in one end to get a better grip, and he began to strike me across the bare buttocks very hard. I winced with the pain of it. Five times he did it, then stopped. I was allowed to pull up my pants, and again The Rat started the same questions. I told him again I didn't know.

Now he forced me to kneel down with my arms over my head, my wrists locked in those irons again. I was told to stay that way, not to let my arms drop at all. Well, for the first hour it wasn't bad; after that, however, my arms began to tire, and I let them relax a bit. Immediately a guard behind saw my arms waver, and he hit me hard across the back of my head. I put my arms up straight again, but now it was as if fifty-pound sacks were hanging on them.

This went on all day Saturday. At three or so I couldn't hold those arms up any longer, and I let them drop. A guard jumped in and hit me with a karate chop on the back of the neck, then a few more times around the head. I fell over. Then Hanoi Fats came in and tied me up again, this time wrapping ropes around my hands, then hiking them up to the back of my head, tying my arms between the elbows and the shoulder sockets so that I could not drop them. I had no choice but to hold them up then.

The rest of the day it was the same treatment. If my arms relaxed even an inch, Hanoi Fats would let me have it. By now I had a cut on my mouth that had begun to bleed. Finally an officer came in, and I recognized Soft-Soap Fairy or The Mystery Man, as we sometimes called him. I yelled at him a little bit. He asked the guard what was wrong, and I showed him the blood I was spitting on the floor. But he took no action. I stayed in that kneeling position with my arms over my head until nine o'clock that night. At nine they let me sit on a stool in the middle of the room. I did not sleep at all that night. The stool had one short leg, one side of the seat was raised higher than the other, only because it was a poor piece of carpentry. One of my rubber sandals had fallen a few feet in front of me. Behind the table in front of me sat The Rat, watching me coldly. When I asked questions, he beat me with that rubber sandal across my face.

So the night passed on that stool, and I tried to ignore the pulsing pain in my face, my mouth, my arms, my shoulders, my legs. The next morning around five, WTG came in and gave me a cigarette and a light. He gave me about ten minutes to smoke it. When I finished I threw the butt into a corner.

Then The Rat came in. "Time for more questions," he said shortly. "If you answer my questions correctly, then I can go down and spend Sunday on the lakes, which I would much rather do. If you do not answer, then I don't care. We'll stay here until you do answer."

So I went through the same painful routine all through Sunday, until nine o'clock that night. I was beaten with a fan belt on ten different occasions on Sunday during the day, about five licks each time. Then at nine it was back on the stool again, the ropes and those heavy irons on my legs beginning to drag on me.

Monday was the same—still no sleep. Came Tuesday and I saw that my knees were infected from kneeling so long on them, and the skin around my Achilles tendons was oozing pus too from where the leg irons rubbed. On Tuesday two guards came in; one I recognized as The Slug, and the other was WTG. It was their day to stay with me and make sure I kept my arms over my head while kneeling down. Each time I would drop my arms after hours of holding them up, they would beat me around the shoulders with a bamboo stick.

Then I began to have hallucinations. I saw that the squares on the concrete floor were about fourteen inches wide. They were solid slabs of concrete, but there was a little indentation and the concrete was pitted. They wanted me to kneel in the places that were pitted, so I moved from square to square, to relieve my knees. I had brought home a piece of Sicilian marble years before which had a few cracks which I had filled with beeswax. Each square of the concrete now seemed to me to be filled with beeswax, and I kept thinking, "This square has twenty-two pounds of beeswax, this square has twenty-four pounds of beeswax, this square has thirty pounds of beeswax."

"Who is on the Zoo escape committee?" The Rat kept asking me.

I tried to tell him there was no such committee in the Zoo. But others who had been tortured already had told them the committee existed.

And so I went on all day—and they started it all over again. I would not give them the escape committee—I felt I had to protect Larry Guarino, Ted Kopfman, and J. J. Connell, who were already suspected by the Vietnamese. I simply would not put the finger on them. But I realized by now that the others who had been tortured had probably told them that we had organized the escape out of the Annex, and this was the confession that they wanted to hear.

Finally, unable to bear the agony of it any longer, I decided to tell them that my room in the Zoo was the source of the escape committee. I had to tell them something, anything, to get some relief. By now I couldn't think, I was hallucinating. I had had no sleep, hardly any food. The pain in my shoulders and my legs was a fire shooting through my body. My face was beaten to a pulp, my mouth was swollen. So I said my room in the Zoo was the source of the escape.

"Who else is going to escape?" The Rat barked at me.

"I am."

"What are you going to take with you?"

"An escape kit . . ."

"What is in it?"

"Rice, iodine, bread, canned meat," I mumbled through my swollen lips.

"Where do you have that supply hidden?"

"In the back of the bath behind the Garage."

So they stopped the interrogation and went to the bath and tore the bath apart looking for the escape supplies. They found nothing. They came back, and I knew they knew I was lying. But I at least had the hour to get some relief.

"You lied," The Rat said flatly. I waited to get hit, but instead he asked, "How do you plan to go out?"

"Through the front door, how else?" I said, and I remembered how Bill Austin and I had taken off that inner door once.

"How do you plan to get through the door?"

"I'll knock it down. . . ."

They stopped again and went out right away and put a large metal hasp on that door to reinforce it. They did this to all the doors, but only on mine did they put a heavy four-by-four beam in addition, which was to be called by the other prisoners "McDaniel's Escape Bar."

But they weren't satisfied with the information I had given them. They kept at me, trying to drag more from me. On the fifth night I thought I could sleep. WTG had said, "Five night sleep," and that apparently had been the policy. But on that fifth night I still was not allowed to sleep. In fact, I was forced to kneel down until past nine o'clock that night, and the officer stayed longer than usual. By then I was running a high temperature of 104° to 105° from the infections in my knees and the oozing wounds on the backs of my heels from those irons. So much came out of those wounds that whenever I moved around in that small room a trail of pus would be left behind along the floor.

On Wednesday the same treatment, beginning with the "setup" cigarette at 5:00 A.M. Then, right on schedule, ten minutes later The Rat came in, and the questions began, the same ones.

By now I had begun competing with the guards in the room, Slug and WTG. In all of the exhaustion, when my mind wouldn't function, when the pain beat a steady rhythm throughout my body, I still rose to the occasion with an insane desire to beat them. I was determined to stand with my arms up higher and longer than they expected. It was foolish, because it was only wearing me down more, the very thing they wanted. So why did I fight them, why was the game spirit coming up again in such a ridiculous place and in such a setting?

"Great day!" His name was Frank L. Mock. He was my high-school coach. I swung on strike three with the bags loaded and he yelled, "Great damn day!" That was the only time I ever heard him drop a bad word, but I never held it against him. Now, in this hour of darkness, his kindly, rough-hewn face floated before me like a balloon.

How many times had we practiced under him? How many times had he put me through my paces? How many times had he drilled me in the fact that playing the game is "all in the winning"? And, as if I might miss the point, he added, "To win isn't everything—actually, it's the only thing."

Every game, every challenge of life was built around that statement for me. The military picked it up and socked it home. You flew to win against the opposing elements of empty space; you flew to win in combat. The American way was to win. "I never saw an American who lost and laughed," General George S. Patton said once. I wouldn't lose. I couldn't lose. I had been drilled to win.

But "winning" was not the issue anymore to many people. Many people had said that about the war; we'd heard it enough on the "box" over Radio Hanoi. It's not a "win" you're after; a "draw" might do. I knew that everybody was talking about the hopelessness of winning this war in Vietnam . . . maybe they were right.

But I couldn't turn it off that easily. I had to hang on to winning, I had to compete, or I was dead in this place. Frank Mock's drive to make me want to win had to count now in the biggest battle of my life. And yet I knew, too, as Grantland Rice put it, "He marks—not that you won or lost —but how you played the game." Frank Mock had inspired me to win but also to put character into the game, to put all I had into it regardless of the outcome. In my senior year

I was to receive a trophy conceived by a concerned citizen for "the man who gave the most to the game." I treasured that reward, but I owe it to Frank Mock for teaching me that big lesson in playing the game.

But how do I play this "game"—locked in the ropes, bleeding, burning up with fever, my life oozing out of broken flesh, my mind so far gone I couldn't concentrate on their questions, could hardly hear them? Yet all of my discipline of the past told me I had to try.

Were there no winners? If that were true, if that philosophy were right, then what was I fighting for in this room? Why didn't I just roll over and die, let it happen?

Pride? Yes, I had it. I played the game and I was proud to be playing. All my life I had found pride in accomplishment, in winning, sometimes even just being out there and competing. I was proud to fly formation with my fellow pilots. I was proud to fly for the United States. I had caught the team spirit—loyalty to cause and country—early in life. Perhaps I wasn't so proud of letting go with bombs on targets; no combat man is. There is nothing to be proud of in inflicting pain and death. But there is something to be proud of in aiding the cause of a people who have no one to care, who have to stand alone. I was proud to be a part of my country's concern to do that. Regardless of what history would say, I could not deny my beliefs—I threw myself into the Vietnam war, because I believed, like my government, in the rightfulness of it and I was proud to play my part. Even if that cause is not a popular one, a man had to take his stand for something, sometime. My Communist captors, the VC, had their cause and they were out to win—to tell them there is no winning in this war would bring laughter. Tell them to learn to be "graceful losers"; they wouldn't understand the statement. For all the bombing we did, they still had squadrons of rolling trucks full of soldiers and equipment. For all our superior fire power, they could still storm barbed wire in human waves. For them, winning was everything—and *their* pride was in even dying to prove it.

So what did I have left in this bloody hole I was in, being

slowly reduced to a broken, beat-up Navy flier? If I were going to live through this, all that had been given to me through my life that counted at all had to be dredged up now. Only the armchair strategists in their wall-to-wall comfort could afford to philosophize about winning or not winning. Pain has a way of focusing for a man, giving him recall of what really matters. With death knocking at the door, a man has time for only one thing: to go out with some kind of honor.

Around noon The Slug was still there watching me. I knew he wanted to get his siesta, but he couldn't, because it was his duty to stay here and watch me, make sure I got it if my arms dropped an inch. And I felt some triumph just from that—because he couldn't leave me and get any shuteye all because he had to be there. And I kept my arms up, jabbing him that way, never giving him the satisfaction.

Then Slug was relieved by a new guard we called Scar-under-the-Eye. He was a short man, about four feet eight inches, with a large, grotesque scar under his right eye. He looked savage and he was. And now I couldn't keep my arms up there, so I relaxed, and he hit me, cuffing me around the head. Finally, after so much of that, I said I had to use the toilet bowl. I had to get relief from that banging around. I had been having bad diarrhea by then anyway, so they let me use it. I took the few minutes on that bowl to rest, and then Scar was on me again. I finally collapsed and fell over on the floor and he grabbed me by the hair and pulled me back upright with a jerk.

Now I felt I had nothing left to resist with. Nothing. I became irrational. I grabbed Scar and started yelling, *"Bao cao!"* all the time hanging on to him. He countered by shoving a dirty rag down my throat. I had had a blindfold on since he had started on me, tight across my nose, which cut off my breathing through the nasal passages. That rag in my throat now cut off my only other source of air. So I grabbed him again in desperation and I managed to shove him up against the wall, even in my leg irons, and immediately I let him go, sensing what I had done. He went tearing out of the room, called seven or eight of his buddies outside, and came charging back in. It seemed as if half the North Vietnamese army was pouring into that cubicle. By then the officers had heard the commotion, and they too had come down to see what was going on. They took the blindfold off, and when they looked at me I could tell they knew they had me. I asked for a cigarette, something to push them off for a few minutes, and they laughed. They thought that perhaps now they had won.

They put me back into the ropes, but this time they tossed another rope over the ceiling beam and ran it through a pulley. Next they pulled the rope and lifted me off the floor, so I was dangling a few feet off the cement. The pain of being hiked up was worse than any I had experienced up until then, all my weight being borne by my already beaten arms and shoulder sockets. Then Jawbone moved up to me and tried to tighten the ropes around my arms further. To do this, he had to drop me on the floor, and while I was standing there, glad for the reprieve from hanging on that pulley, he put his foot up against one of my arms so he could get leverage to tighten the ropes. As he did so I heard the bone crack, even before I felt it—and then the pain hit, stabbing a line of fire up into my brain.

I shouted, panting heavily from the exertion of fighting those ropes, "You've broken my arm," addressing The Rat, who stood watching a few feet away.

"No," he said simply, "we have not broken your arm. *You* have broken your arm." All the time WTG, who had come into the room, was trying to push that exposed bone back into place—a peculiar gesture, as if he were ashamed of its sticking out like that, or perhaps he was trying to ease it back in to save me the pain.

"We will punish step by step," The Rat went on. They would never say "torture." "Until you give us the information we want, we will punish." Then they would try variations like running ropes through my leg irons and pulling my legs in different ways. All the time, the same question. Who was the escape committee? And I kept hanging onto the same answer: "I don't know. We did not have an escape committee in the Zoo." Which was true. The escape was planned over in the Annex, in a nine-man room, but since I was the chief link in the communications network, they knew I had to know who was involved in that. I wondered if I should tell them something . . . anything to get them off me.

On the sixth night, I thought, "Surely tonight I will get some sleep." But they kept me even longer this time, making me kneel on that pitted cement with my arms up. Then it was back on that unbalanced stool, the slaps across my face now and then from The Rat with that tire sandal when I wouldn't talk. Sometimes there were long periods of nothing . . . only the mosquitoes. I watched those mosquitoes come down on my bare legs and their bellies swell with my blood, and then I watched them fall off one by one, too full to fly away. After a while, I noticed a lot of little frogs in the room, hopping here and there. One night in a half doze on that stool I looked down to see the frogs come up and grab the mosquitoes off my leg, their tongues darting out, the wetness of them touching my skin. I did nothing about it; I had neither the strength nor the desire to do anything anyway. It was all a part of a distorted world, a world of life and death, the strong overcoming the weak.

Then I began to go into hallucinations. I mentally unlocked the irons around my ankles, taking off the bar that ran between the two. Now I had them off and began to move my legs. But I still felt I had them on. So for thirty minutes I worked to unlock them again, removing the bar, my mind perfectly clear as to what I was doing. And I would jerk my legs, knowing the irons were off, only to be yanked back to reality as the irons held and sent new pain up my ankles and legs. I kept at it all night, absolutely certain I had those irons off, getting up to walk, falling back again until I wondered if I had the wrong key.

At another point I heard Bing Crosby, singing "White Christmas" in the background, over and over. A chorus filtered in over that, singing "September Song," and I smiled at the words and tried singing along with the chorus. It helped a little.

Once I saw Ken Fleenor through a small window in my room that opened into his. I saw only his head, though, and he had his shirt pulled over it. In that same room I saw Al Runyan running in place, as he used to in the room at the Zoo, and I yelled to him, "Al, let's go out and bathe."

"Just a few minutes more," Al yelled back.

I waited for an hour, anxious to put my hands in the cool water of the shower, so finally I yelled to Al, "I can't wait any longer, I must go." In my hallucination I went out and washed my hands in water, but it had no effect at all, and I continued on into the torn-up night, my hands burning badly. Sometime during the night I found a piece of cloth in the room from which I made a sling to put my broken left arm into and tied it loosely with my teeth, wrapping it around my neck. But I made it too long and the arm hung down too much even then. Once having done it, however, there was no untying it, so I sat there, letting the night wear on, my mind moving in and out of hallucinations, hoping for sleep, trying for sleep, unable to sleep.

The next morning WTG came in with the one cigarette, and I showed him the arm. He said, "Uh," and that was all. The point was that I was not going to get any medical aid until the interrogators were finished with me.

Thursday began. This time it was the ropes again, but now they put cords around my arms, tied wet damp cloths around the cords, and hooked these cords up to a battery. They gave me electric shock treatments on and off, and the pain was blinding, but mercifully I was so tired that it was only another blurring dimension of the pain I already had.

"You tell us now," the same words kept pounding at me from a long way off, "and we will stop."

I remembered Colonel Risner, who had roomed near me earlier, saying that we should take the torture only up to permanent physical damage to ourselves. Then, Risner suggested, give them what they want, then bounce back and come back in the next round to win. And the guards seemed to know that too, because The Rat said, "Permanent damage is being done. You must tell us and then we'll stop."

Yet I couldn't tell them anything. I still felt I should protect Guarino, Kopfman, and Connell. But why? I didn't know, except that I still entertained the idea that to tell was to open the gate on torture for them. Others had put the finger on me, even when I was not in the escape attempt; I was tempted to tell, to follow Risner's wise advice. Was I gaining anything playing the hero like this? All I could look forward to was being grotesquely maimed for life, if I ever got out alive. Maybe it was foolish . . . playing the game . . . competing . . . pride . . . wanting to win . . .

And so more electric shock. For three hours or so the treatment kept on. Once they stopped and put some food on the table, greens and soup, so I knew it had to be noon. The next time they gave me the same ration, it had to be four. I was still going through the ropes and the shock treatment, one jolting jab of voltage, jerking me in spasms, then another.

I felt myself sliding then. I was being beaten, whipped, falling to the point of nothingness. Death would be welcome. I wanted the pain to stop. My mouth was puffy, swollen, and my face was burning from the slaps from the guards with their rubber sandals. I was conscious of a guard sitting in front of me with his fan belt lightly striking me across the nose, tantalizing me. My will to hold on was dissolving.

Then I became aware that I wasn't going to come through this after all. I had drawn on all the reserves I had of pride, optimism, and the will to compete in this macabre game with my guards, the things I thought would carry me through. I had allowed hate for them to enter, for hatred fanned the flames of my determination to win. But I was miserably broken for all of that. I was bleeding, wracked with fever, my mind numbed by the electric shock, in and out of nightmarish hallucinations. Suddenly I was not a U.S. Navy flyer at all; I was not a patriot at this point, and being an American meant nothing in the reality of the moment. I was simply a human being sliding further and further toward death, and there was nothing at all to reach out for anymore, within or without.

I thought of God then. In all this time, I had kept my mind on the pain that was coming in the next second, on bracing myself to outwit my guards, to dig in a little deeper to prevent myself from telling them anything. I was fighting a war in that room, trying to plan each move, trying to stand tall like a good military man. Now I sensed I was losing for all of that, and I felt I was losing whatever I had of God as well. Was faith all a myth then? I had prayed, quoted Scripture, tried to live up to what I thought God would have of me—but what had I to show for it now? Where was that verse, the promise of Christ, that said, "Lo, I am with you always"? Where was the deliverance? *Where was He?* I had fought with all I had and lost—now was I going to lose the knowledge of God too?

I thought maybe I should try quoting more verses to remind God where I was, who I was, but none came. And I realized suddenly then that all the calling up of Scripture, all those repetitions of the Beatitudes, the Twenty-third Psalm, the prayers, maybe all of those had been meant to get God over to my side, to prevent the agony I was now in. That sense of the incompleteness of Christ in my life that I had felt even in the doing of all that, that big fragment of the unknown about God in my life, was it only now coming home? Would it only now dawn on me with new reality? I saw my life all over again in a few seconds—from that conversion experience in college all the way through to shootdown. In all that time, I had assumed Christ was in me, making of me a kind of model person in morality, good citizenship, love of country, family, and all the rest of it. But now I was struck with the fact that I had not entered into the sufferings of Christ in all that time. I had lived on the "good times" of Christianity, but I had never been tested by pain, as He had been, and the dimension missing in my life was tied directly to that.

In my befogged mind, and with the pulse of pain through

me, I sensed that maybe God was trying to say something to me—that maybe there was something bigger, more real, more valuable than simply being the eternal optimist or the one who "gave the most to the game." Had I really given the most? Up to now, I knew I hadn't. It struck me then that God must have led me here, let me get shot down, that I might now enter into the totality of what it was all about to be in Him.

I tried to think it through while the pain kept up that mocking kind of rhythm in my body, telling me there was nothing to be gained from that kind of thinking either. But I remembered back in Heartbreak Hotel in Hanoi in 1967, at the height of my three-day torture, hearing church bells coming from somewhere in downtown Hanoi. I remembered hearing them at the very height of my pain and darkness then. I remembered then how it seemed that God was saying something to me in those soft bells, that he was not far away from me, that there was no pain or darkness so great that He would be outside it. I remembered what that had meant then, the hope it had given me, the renewed will to hang on.

There were no bells now, however, and I was worse off than I had been back there. I strained to hear those bells again, desperately wanting some evidence that God cared, that He was here with me in this place. I knew that if He didn't do something, reveal something of Himself to me, I could not make it. And, in my feeble way again, I said, "Lord . . . it's all Yours . . . whatever this means, whatever it is supposed to accomplish in me, whatever You have in mind now with all of this, it's all Yours. . . ."

That was all I could say. That was all I had the mental strength to frame. I knew it wasn't much, but I meant it. It was the first time I had ever prayed so straight, so directly, so meaningfully. Whatever "commitment" I had given to Him up until then had never brought from me a prayer of surrender like that. I was totally willing now to accept whatever He had in mind, whereas all the time of my life up to this point had been spent reminding God that I was measuring up to Him and therefore He would make sure I never got beyond my depth.

It was a strange prayer for me, yet so absolutely right—even in my mind that could not fully focus on my words. But there wasn't a lot of time right then to dwell on it, because I was conscious of the guard there, waiting for the next slap . . . and yet there was something that preoccupied me even in that prayer, something that lifted the weight of fear from me. I didn't know what that prayer was supposed to accomplish for me. Nothing at all miraculous happened, and I wasn't really expecting anything.

But, in the next minute or so, I became aware of the fact that the ropes were being taken off my arms. The wet cords wrapped around my bare chest were removed. I remained there on my knees a long time, waiting, wondering, my eyes half shut. I kept saying to myself that there must be something worse coming. There was no reason for them to release me like this. They had already killed one prisoner in torture, and I was practically gone now, so there was no reason for them to let up on me. But they did! I was not hallucinating now. I checked to be sure. Yes, I was out of those ropes. My arms were numb and there was pain, but I was free! How? Why? I waited for some explanation from them, from The Rat or Hanoi Fats or WTG. None came. And, as I fell forward, too weak to stay kneeling, dropping down into my own blood and wastes, it suddenly seemed that the fifteen-watt bulb was turning on a glow of warmth within me. It was God. It had to be. I was alone, all the grim horrors of the past days and nights still with me, but now I had a moment of peace. I didn't know how to absorb the immensity of the moment, the sheer dimension of it, the mystery of it, yes —or the reality of it as well.

I didn't know how long I lay there drawing on that aura of the presence of God. After a while, however, I began to take stock. I found I had lost control of my hands completely. They just dangled down, unfeeling, unmoving to my will. The ropes had paralyzed the nerves in them, and there was no way I could get them to move; it would remain so for a long time. It was going on evening, and I saw through my blurred vision that they had put rations on the table for me. No one was in the room yet. I saw the bowl of greens, the half loaf of bread, the bowl of watery rice soup. It was like manna from heaven! But I did not have the physical ability to reach that food. Without my hands I couldn't do much. So I moved over inch by inch, and very slowly, painfully, pulled myself up to that table, still in leg irons, my badly broken arm hanging out at a peculiar angle from my side. I pushed myself up on my hands that could not feel, dipped my mouth into the soup, and began lapping it up like a dog. I did the same with the greens. It was slow, but I kept at it, because I knew I had to have that energy in order to go on. In between chewing in my swollen mouth, I thought of the provision of God, the wonder of it, the miracle of it.

Finished eating, I began to call for medical attention. The guard stepped in and simply said, "When you tell us what we want, you will get medical attention."

So it was the same story with them—nothing changed. But I was wrong. That night, seven or eight days after I had gone into torture, they let me go to the bath. To the bath! I was astounded. By that time I smelled awful, and I walked in a stoop, trying to ease the pains throughout my body. The bath for them was to get me clean so they could put medicine on me. I couldn't figure out their concern to keep infection off, but it may have been that face-saving trait of theirs again. I couldn't come out of torture with oozing pus all over my body, and I was not "allowed" to die either; they were pushing me as far as they could without allowing me to succumb. This face-saving was maddening, but beyond that I knew God had to be in that too, and it gave me a new view of things—they weren't out of control now, and whatever they were doing was subject as much to Him as their own sense of personal image.

When I went to the bath, I couldn't handle the soap with my hands. I could not wash my own clothes either, so I managed to drop them off, get them into a tub of water, and stepped on them with my feet. But when I tried to bathe, I dropped the soap ten or fifteen times. Meanwhile, WTG kept rushing me. I did my best and finished, not really doing much but getting wet. But when I went to pull on my pants, the drawstring came out of one side and disappeared inside the loop of the waist. There was no way I could get it back out in order to tie it, not with my hands. So WTG promptly started beating me again. When he stopped, I would try to get that string out again, and still my hands wouldn't work. WTG knew the condition of my hands, but he wouldn't pull that string out for me; instead, he kept on beating me. Finally he said, "Now we go," and I managed to keep my elbows flush up against my waist to hold those pants up, although my one broken arm didn't help much. When we got back to the room, he put some red liquid on my wounds, and I counted over thirty-eight of them. The red stuff was like a Merthiolate that scabbed over the wound in a hurry and prevented infection.

Then he put me back into the leg irons because I had not fixed my pants, and jerked me around with those irons, so that terrible spasms of pain ran through my legs and back. Finished with jerking me around, he moved out the door, pausing to say, "Queekly!" meaning I better hurry up and get that drawstring out of the hole it was in and tie my pants properly.

I didn't know how to do it now anymore than I had before. Finally I reached down with my teeth and bit three holes in the loops in the pants and got the drawstring through those holes, and finally tied it together with my teeth. When WTG came back, he saw it was tied, though he could not see the holes I had made in the loops to do it. Satisfied, he left, and my pants hung together—rather precariously, but they hung.

Friday came, and I faced it with a little more strength. God was here; that I was positive of now. I could face what was coming with a new sense of hope. But, almost as if they knew, the guards gave me my severest beating. I was beaten regularly by a two-man relay team with more than 120 licks with that fan belt on my bare buttocks. And after thirty licks or so, they would stop and put a watery, wintergreen-smelling substance on my buttocks, which had by now turned to hamburger. All of this, again, was to keep infection down. It was crazy—if I died in here, it seemed they wanted to be sure that no one would find any infection in my body. By now I was passing blood in my urine and through my anus, and that meant there were internal injuries. My eardrum had ruptured when they struck me across the head with my own shoe, and it too was oozing blood.

They continued to beat me that way until I thought I would go out of my mind with the pain. I said, "Okay, I'll tell you, stop." And they stopped. I took the few minutes while they waited just to get my breath and allow the pain to dissipate a little and then I said, "I don't have any answers."

So back to the beating. Then, knowing I couldn't go on anymore, that there just wasn't enough left in me to take it, I said, "Okay, I'll tell you." This time they hung over me, not allowing me time to fake it, and I gave them some names—but not the names they wanted me to confirm. I just told them the names of the senior officers in the building, and that I was the escape committee, nobody else. For some reason, they accepted that; and again, God must have been in it, because I did not confirm any of the information other tortured prisoners had given, and I had not given any names of the actual escape committee.

That Friday night I slept for the first time in a week. I was mistaken to think the interrogations were over or even the torture. But, as I slept, it was a sleep of assurance—God was not far outside this hell. If I had to go on with this nightmare, then I was sure He was with me. Nothing else mattered.

8

Fourth Down—and Goal to Go

SATURDAY. I WOKE TO LOOK AT MY LEGS. They had swollen up grotesquely. I could bury my fist in my right leg, it was so swollen and soft. The wounds from kneeling on the cement were still infected, and my right thigh was swollen. The Achilles tendon on my left leg was fiery red and still oozing pus.

That day there was no torture on the agenda. Instead, a young Vietnamese medical officer came in, a man we called Reggie. He took one look at my wounds and was greatly agitated; he went out and got the doctor immediately. The doctor washed me up, gave me penicillin and sulfa tablets and bandaged the worst of my wounds.

Later that day I was told I could go back to my room, but that order came from a different officer, one who had gold teeth whom we referred to as The Snake. "But," he said, "you must not communicate." I told him I would not, and I meant it. I had had it bucking the rules on that score—at least I thought I had at the time.

The reason they let me go back to my room was that they couldn't get the leg irons back on my swollen ankles. The rule was that you couldn't stay in the Coop without leg irons on. So I went back to the Garage, and the sixteen men in that complex watched me come back, bent, hardly able to walk, my face torn apart—and none of them recognized me. Since I had lost thirty-five to forty pounds, it was understandable. I was put into a room by myself, and that bar was put across my door—"McDaniel's Escape Bar"—just to make sure. The front windows had been bricked up since the escape and the vents as well. I was made to lie down on a bunk away from the wall to the next room, and a guard watched me all night to be sure I did not communicate.

There was no way for me to communicate anyway. With my hands dangling useless, I couldn't even get my mosquito net down over me, so I slept all night without it, which made it easier on the guard watching me. I kept hearing the people all night tapping on the wall next door, trying to get word from me, and they did not know the guard was there watching me and listening. I ignored it until the next morning when I went to use the toilet bowl, and out of sight of the guard there, I tapped on the wall, "Much torture. See you." That's all I did, all I dared to do.

It was 7:30 Sunday morning now, and the guard gave me my cigarette. I smoked it; it was comforting now in my pain—anyway, I figured it was the height of optimism to worry about dying of lung cancer in my condition. I thought the interrogations were over now, but a little while later the guard came, opened my door, and gave me the chop-on-the-wrist sign that I was to suit up. It was back to the Coop again.

They didn't do much to me. I was made to stand in the corner, my arms raised above my head. Sunday night I went back to my room, and Monday morning it was back to interrogation again. Again they wanted that information on the escape committee; now they were not satisfied with my answers. But I would not, and could not, come up with any more than I had. There just wasn't anything more to give.

On the thirteenth day I had to put on one leg iron, since it finally fit over my left ankle, but the other still would not go on over the swelling. On the fourteenth day I was moved into the Carriage House in the Zoo, because they wanted to use the interrogation room to interrogate other prisoners. I was alone now and began to feel the heavy clamp of depression coming down hard on me. Had God led me out of one point of suffering to allow me to die slowly now in isolation? I began to doubt again the deliverance of God at that moment in torture. My body was pretty well beaten up, and I knew I could not survive that and being alone too. Besides the loss of my hands, my broken arm—the bone having been clumsily shoved back under the protruding skin by one of the medics during those long days in torture—a face beaten raw, my buttocks hurting so badly I could hardly sit down, I suddenly began to have real problems controlling my bowels. I couldn't get to the bowl, so I went all over the floor, and I had no way to clean up, no rags or anything. So I had to try to get it up with my hands; it was a messy business at best. I was still passing blood in my urine and through my rectum. And my punctured ear was still draining and giving me equilibrium problems. *How much did a man have to suffer to know Christ in His suffering?*

The Rat visited me there one day to ask if I was better and ready to make a tape. Earlier, four days after release from torture, a VC doctor had worked on my broken arm and, after a lot of painful pulling and squeezing, told me it was the best that could be done. And that's the way it was left; the fact that the bone knitted together by itself in the next few months was no credit to them, but the arm was to remain at a peculiar angle for the months and years to come.

Anyway, The Rat didn't even ask about my medical needs but began to shift his line from information on communications and escape to a demand that I repent of my crime in communicating and apologize to the camp commander. He finally said, "Are you prepared to do some concrete acts?"

I said, "I will wash clothes, sweep—"

"No, I said I want you to do some concrete acts."

"I will mix concrete too," I said.

"You do not understand. You must agree to do concrete acts."

So they took me back into interrogation again, and I didn't think I could take any more of it. I felt alone now, more so than at any other time. I felt forsaken. I had already taken all they could throw at me, and had given them very little for it. Now I knew what depression was, depression so deep that I could not even pray, could not think of my family. My thirteenth wedding anniversary slipped by without my remembering. My mind went into a total neutral, a kind of withdrawal, and it seemed that nothing could pull me out.

That same day the turnkey came, took off my leg irons, and led me back into interrogation. "You must make this tape," The Rabbit said. "If you do, you can ask for special medicine and food."

"I will not ask," I said. "If you are going to give it to me, you must give, but I will not ask."

"You know that we can force you to make this tape?" The Rabbit snapped. "We can force you to do anything."

"Yes, I know you can force me . . . then you will have to force me. . . ."

"But we will not force you," Rabbit said then in a remarkable statement that I was to remember later. "You must do it on your own, you must be willing. Because if we force you, we will look bad in the eyes of the world."

Well, it wasn't that important an issue, and I knew it. A simple apology saying I was a bad boy probably would be all that was required. But they also wanted to make sure I put in that tape that I had received "humane and lenient treatment." That would get them off the hook; perhaps someone in the top echelon in Hanoi was asking them about the torture. So I made the tape, but I made it in my own way: "During the past two weeks I have had many sleepless nights to ponder my so-called crime of communication, and when I return to my room I will fully understand the meaning of the Democratic Republic of Vietnam's humane and lenient treatment. I extend my heartfelt apology to the camp commander."

They didn't like that bit about "many sleepless nights to ponder" and the fact I did it in a monotone, which to The

Rabbit sounded sad. It *was* sad, because that was how I felt right then. I had to do it over and, he said, "You must sound happy. You will be punished more if you don't sound happy." So I made another tape, and on the end of it I added, "This is true to the best of my ability considering my present condition." That last phrase slipped by Rabbit, but anybody with discernment on the outside listening to that would catch the meaning of it.

It was done. I felt I had to give them something anyway, and it wasn't much that they received. I was so sick and so weak that nothing really mattered, and I knew what they could do to me if I held out to the final jot—I had heard of others who had done so, and they had landed in solitary confinement where they had died slowly, little by little. I knew they were contemplating this end for me, because they did not want others to see what I had gone through, thereby losing face again. If they threw me in a room alone to die, nobody would see. In the long run, then, the tape was a cheap price to pay, since they did not get me to condemn my country or harm other prisoners.

Having made the tape, I was put back in my lonely cell. I began to despair more and more often that I would never see the other prisoners again. I was alone, cut off, left to die piece by piece in the loneliness and depression. I knew the other prisoners had their problems too, and it wasn't for them to worry about me. But the more the time went by, and the contemplation of isolation grew on me, the more I kept asking God the "why" of all this.

Again, the Lord was ahead of me: one day the guards moved me from the Carriage House to a building called the Stable. I figured it would just be another isolation cell. But when I walked in I got the happiest surprise of my life. Standing inside was Lieutenant Commander Windy Rivers. I was overjoyed! And he was speechless when he saw me. Ron Bliss, his roommate, said that I looked like a specter out of hell—eyes sunken, skin beginning to show jaundice, stooped over, hands dangling. Immediately they began to do what they could for me. They fed me, shaved me, washed me. I was overwhelmed. God had not only taken me out of solitary, but He had put me with friends who cared. In that same building there were others who were outstanding Christians who communicated their concern for me, constantly assuring me that all would be well, telling me they were praying for me. I could never have dreamed that I could have been placed in so perfect a place for healing in both my body and my wounded spirit.

For instance, Rivers and Bliss soon found out that I could not sit on a toilet bowl very well because the rusty edge that was a feature of camp toilet bowls dug sharply into my raw buttocks. Windy suggested I put my rubber tire sandal on the lid as I sat down. I did so, and it worked a few times; but, since my hands wouldn't function at all, one day I let the sandal fall into the bowl and it sank out of sight. Ron Bliss came over and reached in and pulled it out. That had to be the epitome of dedication of one prisoner for another, and it was these Christian acts, rooted in their faith, that built a whole new camaraderie that got us all through each day. But, more than that, for me it was a beautiful touch of God, for He kept telling me in that way that He was not far outside, even as He had showed me in torture.

I hadn't been very long in the Stable when they asked me if they could communicate to the next room. I was a bit nervous about that, because I had already taken enough in torture for communicating, but I said, "Okay, but make it quick." They did, tapping out that I had been through torture and was in bad condition. The guards, I was sure, heard them, but they didn't interrupt; they wanted the whole camp to know what I had gone through so that the rest of the prisoners would think twice about breaking the communication rule or trying any more escapes.

The next day the door opened again and I went back into interrogation. Each time I was tightening up more, my mind refusing to accept any more of it. Again they wanted that tape about "humane and lenient treatment" done over. I did, dragging it out, saying only that I had two meals a day and three cigarettes. Of course, it wasn't enough, so I was down on my knees again, my hands in the air, and those long hours of increasing agony, confusion, even despair.

My roommates knew what I was going through but could do nothing for me. Every morning it was the same. I would hear the key in the lock, and my stomach would tighten up, hoping it would not be for me. Then the guard would stick his head in and say, "Moc," and I would get up without a word and go out.

During this time, for weeks on end, my faith faltered badly. We heard a couple of really bad antiwar statements that had been made by two other prisoners, and that didn't help any. Meanwhile, I was still passing blood, and after about two weeks in the Stable I got very sick, so sick that they had to pour medicine in me for fifteen days to get me propped up again. They even gave me some milk. When in interrogation on my knees a Vietnamese medical orderly would come in and get me up to give me medicine. It was maddening. The guards kept inflicting wounds—but at the same time they made sure I had medicine so I would not die.

On July 29 I moved out of the Stable over to the building we called the Pigsty. I moved in with Jack Van Loan, along with Everett Southwick and Doug Burns. All three were Christians. Again God was with me moving me in with them; they gave me new confidence as they ministered to me with a compassion that went beyond all bounds. Van Loan worked on my hands for two hours every day until I could feel something in them again. The others shared the chores of feeding me, washing me, shaving me. I began to walk around more and one day even managed to shave myself.

One night we had our evening prayers together. As I sat listening to the others talk, I began to sense the wonder of God's handiwork in me in the last few weeks. Since the moment at the very height of my despair in torture when the Lord had heard my feeble prayer of surrender, I had seen some beautiful gestures from Him through my roommates. Not only was I miraculously spared from death in torture, I had been delivered from isolation and put into the hands of men who cared for me and healed me. I was beginning to know finally what the suffering of Christ meant—but I was also beginning to know the benediction of God on my life.

When I was asked to pray, then, I didn't know what to say specifically, but suddenly I sensed the burden deep within and said, "I'd like to pray for our Vietnamese guards." Nobody said anything. Maybe it was a bit of a shock. After I'd taken everything they could throw at me in torture, shouldn't the guards have been the last recipients of prayer I would consider? But then again, as I prayed, I knew the other men were entering in with me. I had lost my hatred for my captors. I had once hated them for what they were doing to me in torture, but now I could sit here, knowing fully they could do it to me again, and yet I felt the need to pray for them. There never was any doubt as I prayed that Christ had done something in my life . . . something profound, something very deep, something meaningful that would follow me all my days. There was no question that I had been perfected in my faith through what I had suffered. Perfected to the point that my view of a good many things had changed—even that of my VC jailers. I no longer regretted the time in torture, nor did I feel that every quiz or interrogation session was evidence of God's letting me down. Each incident now was building in me a new sensitivity to God and all who were around me.

Later I shared with Van Loan and the others what the camp commander, Rabbit, had said about the fact that they could not force us to say things on tape because they would look bad in the eyes of the world. They agreed that the statement was not typical of the Vietnamese; it was a reversal of policy. They agreed with me, too, that there must be pressure coming down from the top in Hanoi, and maybe it meant they would have to ease up as a result.

Ease up they did. I did not go back into torture for days. The security tightened, however; the vents were cemented in and the walls were built higher around us. It was harder now to communicate, but we still managed to get our messages through, although the refinishing of our bathroom and courtyard walls meant we had no holes for passing the notes.

I began to recover slowly, my ear continuing to drain for eighteen months. My arm, though bent back into some reasonable shape, would never really be the same again. But the pressure of the torture was easing, and I am sure that the people in the States demanding better treatment for us have to get the credit.

We didn't know how much work the POW wives were doing with their persistent efforts to get better treatment for us, but sometimes new shoot-downs brought us up to date. I had no idea how much Dorothy was involved—that she was playing a key role in the organization of POW wives back in Virginia Beach.

In October 1969 we began to get better food, a definite signal that something was changing for the better. Now they gave us bread most of the time with our soup. We were getting canned meat at times, sometimes candy. Food packages were coming through finally, and now the Vietnamese were not holding them back on us so much. We began to see odd attempts at beautification for our camp. Sometime previously, during the heavy bombing raids of 1968, the camp commander named Spot had moved a half-track armored truck into the compound just in case. It sat there a long time, nobody bothering to move it. When the camp received a new coat of whitewash later, the truck got a dose of it too so that it blended right into the landscape. After a while, the guards stripped the truck down, taking off the tires, and then it sat there—a grim-looking skeleton, baking in the sun, turning rusty with the rains. Sometimes the guards would climb into the cab and pretend they were driving it, like little kids playing army.

One day, in the new beautification program in 1969, Rabbit came to one of the American officers and asked what could be done, in his opinion, to make the camp look more presentable. After the American recovered from the shock of being asked, he said, "Well, you can do something about that old truck sitting out there . . . at least you can bury it."

133

Rabbit turned and looked at the useless vehicle, not sure how that could have anything to do with an improvement, but he went off and brought back fifteen guards with picks and shovels. In a few hours they had dug a hole next to that truck and pushed it in. In another few minutes the truck was buried. And that was that.

I finally was permitted to write my first letter home in late 1969. It was a glorious experience to communicate with Dorothy after all this time. But it was hard to know what to say and what not to say. I simply wrote:

> *Dearest Dorothy, Mike, David, Leslie—*
>   My health is good in all respects. No permanent injuries. You are my inspiration. Children—work, study, and play hard. Help each other and Mommy. Be strong for our reunion. Invest savings in mutual funds and stocks. Your decisions are mine, Dorothy. I love you deeply.
>
> *Eugene*

Mentioning mutual funds and stocks was to be a source of humor later, but right then I wanted my family to be protected by the best means. I was optimistic then about that reunion, because the Vietnamese were changing their treatment of us for the better. Better food and at least some attempts at giving medical attention—which was nothing more than handing out vitamin pills for infections or feeding bananas to those with high blood pressure, the reasons for which I never could figure out—at least it indicated something had to be going on at the Peace Talks in Paris. More, it meant the united efforts of the POW wives at home were again beginning to tell on the commanders in Hanoi. But there were also definite signs of another phase: There were more attempts to make a good propaganda front for that "humane and lenient treatment" to counteract the bad press the VC were getting about how they treated us. This was to begin a new challenge for us—how to outwit the VC attempts to dress up our activities as reinforcement for their image as kind jailers. After taking two years and more of the pressure to resist them in giving information, having taken all they could throw at us in terms of punishment, restriction, and harassment, we were not about to be used in this way. The letters from home indicated that the concern for us POWs was building. This gave us that extra boost to dig in against our captors on this new front.

I sensed the enemy's desire to get us to go along with their new face-saving attempts. We knew that a few prisoners were cooperating—going downtown to Hanoi and giving statements to the American antiwar delegations who were visiting there. The way I figured it, each man had to face his own conscience on that. As we came closer together, however, as our rooms began to expand to nine and fifteen men, we began to move more as a group, to unite and resist this kind of thing.

By the fall of 1969 the word had gotten out in the Zoo and the Annex that I had been through a severe torture and had come through. Men began to communicate with me, asking me how it was, how I took it. For me to come through meant that they might be able to, too. Others who had been through it passed on their encouragement—this system could be beaten. The North Vietnamese had tried to break us, and we were yet able to stand. And in a way we had won, because our treatment was better now than before we had gone into the leg irons and the ropes.

But I never let the others forget what God had done for me in the torture, that I had come out with an entirely new dimension in faith and commitment. As a result, I was asked to lead in Sunday-morning devotions in our room late in 1969. I didn't know a lot about the Bible even then, but I had proven a lot of things about God's deliverance in those pain-filled hours of torture. I found that the others in the room listened attentively when I spoke about God and His presence with us and the optimism that is tied to faith that can make the big difference. Once I even prayed for my Vietnamese guards, like Slug and WTG, because I felt no enmity toward them, no hate. Some of the men in the room couldn't understand that and asked me how I could pray like that. I simply said it was of God—and there was no other way to explain it.

Once when I had received a package from Dorothy that contained some candy, I had opened it in my room, and I offered a piece to Jawbone, the guard who had been so vicious toward us in his harassment. He looked shocked that I would actually make such a gesture. For a long time he just stared at me, then slowly looked around to make sure no one else of his companions was looking, since it was a rule they could accept nothing from us. Finally he took it.

In that act of taking, maybe something happened between us. I didn't know either how I could make that kind of gesture toward one who had inflicted such pain on me, but it could only be God in me, something of the wonder of Him that had passed through me in the hours of my suffering in those long dark nights.

Meanwhile, one of the first clear acts of trying to demonstrate a "humane and lenient treatment" to those American delegations visiting Hanoi and to the world press in general was when Rabbit formed a choir from among our two camps. The Rabbit prided himself on being fluent in the English language and on being one of the boys, so he got one man from each building and passed out a lot of rumors, good ones, to kind of prop us all up.

"I tell you these things and am allowing you to communicate these things," he told that select group for the choir. "I am telling you these things, because I know you will go back to your rooms and communicate them. Besides, I already know your communications system is so good that you know when I have a headache before I do."

We got that message all right, and it was a tremendous statement, an acknowledgment that we did have something so important going on that even the camp commander would admit it.

Rabbit told our choir that things would improve, that a new camp was being built out by the mountains, that we would get more outside time, more roommates, and other benefits. These things began to come to pass.

In the Pigsty, where I was living, there were eleven rooms. Earlier they had put a wall right down the center of the building to make these small confining rooms to keep us isolated as much as possible. Then in December 1969 they took the wall down, so we now had twice as much space and gained three more roommates—which meant we could enjoy some variety in our conversations.

We also began to get a third dish during the day, some beans and, later, some soybean curd. And on that Christmas in 1969 there was, of all things, a church service convened by the North Vietnamese. Those of us who had been tortured were forced to attend this service, so I went, but it was the only one I went to which the Vietnamese "sponsored." I found out that it was a propaganda stunt. We were photographed in that service, put on film, and it was all a part of the Vietnamese attempt to disprove any reports of torture or bad treatment. Their intent, too, of course, was to show the world that we could have our own church services. But only a limited number were allowed to go to this service, which meant that the Vietnamese did not trust us, as a group, to be together very long.

They were right. During that service, while the "preacher," who was a North Vietnamese, rattled on about U.S. imperialism and U.S. warmongers, I noticed that I was sitting across from Lieutenant Commander Dale Doss. Doss was in my squadron when I was shot down, and there he was, the first time I'd known he was shot down. Surely Dale had seen my wife, I thought; so we talked throughout the service, not bothering to pay attention to the "preacher."

Several days later I asked Rabbit if he would let me visit with Doss, who could tell me about my family, and he said, "You have a very bad attitude, and I think you talked too much the other night during the church service." Well, Rabbit had been the interpreter that night on the platform, but his eyes hadn't missed a thing.

So our "choir" sang, practiced, and moved around a lot. They sang "September Song" for me, which had a lot of meaning for me now, even more than before. And every time the choir sang, the men communicated something to us or to the others—in their choice of songs, gestures, or whatever. While the Vietnamese were getting propaganda out of this, then, the choir in the meantime was doing the very thing the VC had tortured us for so many times. So the spirit to stay ahead of the enemy never died, no matter what the context, no matter what the treatment—and maybe there was an even greater attempt to stay ahead now because the Vietnamese were trying so hard to make us give them a good image.

Then The Rabbit figured on another image-building idea: In early 1970 he started an art program. They took prisoners downtown to the art museum. Always the VC would make sure one man in the room stayed behind, so that, if the others tried an escape, they would come back and sweat out of the remaining prisoner the details of how it was done. So they dressed up these men in Vietnamese suits with special hats, big shoes, and took them to the museum. The purpose, again, was to show the world's press that the prisoners were allowed to pursue art, and they even displayed some of the prisoners' "art," some of which the men did, but most of which was that of the Vietnamese themselves. I was never asked to do this, because I did not draw or paint, and any attempt on their part to get me to do it was frustrating to them.

In July 1970 the Zoo Annex was closed and the men in there were moved up to a new compound called Camp Faith, which had been built as a model POW camp to show the world that the North Vietnamese were very humane as captors. In September we were moved out of the Zoo to Camp Faith. Oddly enough, it was done in the usual style of the Vietnamese, keeping us from seeing anything of the outside and as little as possible of each other.

As we boarded the bus that was to take us to the new camp, we saw that they had put blankets over the windows so we could not see out. We were handcuffed to the seats, of course. If that bus turned over, there was no way for us to get out, but that was the least of their worries. And considering the roads we had to travel, none of us could afford even to think about it. Again we were stuffed into that vehicle like animals; as far as they were concerned, that was all we were anyway. They had tacked up the blankets over the windows with twenty-penny nails, and it was a new bus, at that, so the interior was completely ruined by that kind of treatment. But at least we would see everybody in the bus, and that was the first experience I was to have of being with more than two or three prisoners, nine at the most, at any time in my imprisonment to date.

Well, I soon found out why almost sixty of us rode together. When we arrived at Camp Faith, all of us in that bus were to share the same compound. I was assigned to a twenty-man room, and we had four other rooms with various numbers of people which totaled up to fifty-seven in the compound. We had more time outside at least, about two and a half hours. This helped, and it was a part of their program to show lenient treatment to the prisoners, all a part of trying to save face.

Now we could meet prisoners out in the courtyard. No longer did we have to stick to that peephole in the door to see out and to try to identify someone across the walkway. It was enjoyable to move from one man to another; if I didn't like the conversation in one place I could move on. It was strange after three years of isolation, but it was most exhilarating too.

As we came together in larger groups, it also compounded our discipline problems. As the treatment got better, our discipline seemed to vanish. It was the old story about adversity drawing us closer, prosperity making us independent and more selfish. It was because of the growing unrest of being thrown together, where diverse personalities could play more easily on each other's nerves, that we had to organize more games. The Vietnamese were now giving us permission to boil water for coffee—when we had it, which was not very often. They began building a Ping-Pong table for us. Again, it was not because they had become suddenly concerned about us, but because American delegations were coming to take a look at the American prisoners and our treatment.

Camp Faith was made up of four compounds, and two of them were separated by a few hundred yards. Now we had water pipes on which to tap our code, and soup pots under which to send our notes. Our taps could reach fellow prisoners a quarter of a mile away using those water pipes, so we always stayed in touch.

The North Vietnamese, meanwhile, continued to soft-soap us. The camp commander came around one day and said, "You will no longer have to bow. We permit you to just nod your head in a greeting; you don't have to bow." Well, we did neither, but they did force us to say, "Good morning." Most of us never even did that, because we felt it too was an insult. After all we had taken from them, we did not figure we owed them anything in the way of a greeting. And this was another way of building the tension, their way of trying to force us to their control even while they made the attempt to put on the big show of humane treatment for us. We never knew how to read the faces of our guards now. When they laughed, we thought it meant things were better; but we found that the opposite sometimes was true. Smiling might mean things were going well for them in the war. When they were frowning, we would get more food, so we realized there was no reliable way to read them.

But there was a reason for everything there. If the food got better, we knew someone was leaning on somebody somewhere—probably at home or in Paris. I was often called a "gastropolitician" because I could tell the change in the war or the Peace Talks just by the menu. And when that food improved—more rice, bread, meat, other goodies—we would say, "Well, roll 'em up, we'll be going home soon." And whenever the Vietnamese thought we were going home, things would get better. But then three weeks or so would pass, and we'd be back to the spare rations again—and to the usual harassments.

It was in Camp Faith that we began to sense we had to

do something extravagant in order to occupy ourselves. By now many of the men had been in prison since 1965, and with no real hope that we would be getting out soon—other than my usual "hope-mongering"—and the length of their imprisonment had begun to get to them. Many became belligerent to the VC, talking back to them and of course bringing reprisals. This would mean a cut in rations, back to the harassment, maybe more quizzes.

It was in this atmosphere of growing tension, and the real fear that some of the men might try to organize an escape or even storm the walls, that we began what was to be called "Hanoi University." We organized classes under the instruction of men who we found were experts in a particular field —or who, if not so expert, had enough knowledge to put together a course anyway. Four nights a week we had those classes, two classes a night maybe an hour or so long. By the time we had fully organized, we were teaching fifty-five to sixty different subjects, among them French, Spanish, German, Russian, history, and real estate. In fact, I even taught a three-month seminar in love and marriage.

In my love and marriage seminar, I had twenty-five or so prisoners attending, single men and married alike. In our once-a-week meeting I would take a young couple through courtship, then into marriage; plan their wedding and number of children; show them how to raise the children through their teens. We discussed how we would adjust when we got home, if for example we found our wives had become alcoholics in our absence. Or what would we do if our wives had remarried? Or supposing they had been unfaithful? These possibilities were real ones, which lurked in the back of every man's mind. Sometimes the uncertainty would play on them, depress them, make them overanxious. By giving this class, I was able to provide something for them to grab onto, to prepare them for that possible return home, and to brace them for whatever they might find.

The way we learned Russian was by taking the labels off Russian tins of fish and meat given in our rations. The same with French. We did have some men fluent in these languages, but the "homework" between classes was to memorize the words on the labels to keep our minds busy in the lull periods.

One night a week was devoted to a travelogue. One man would be appointed to take us through his state, telling us all about the various aspects of it, from agriculture to high-ways, cities, manufacturing, famous tourist sites, etc. Some nights we would reproduce old movies by narrating them as best we could—the actors, the plots, the whole thing. If we forgot the plot, we'd make up our own, and this would some-times be hilarious.

I still believe I learned more in those classes than I did in college at home; in camp, the motivation was there. Besides that, 80 percent of the prisoners were college graduates; they were used to learning; and a good 15 to 20 percent of them had advanced degrees in all kinds of major concentrations.

We even had men capable of teaching classes on basket weaving; men who had done term papers on such things as the Warsaw Pact; others who were authorities on the Suez Canal, on insurance, on sports. We had a Marine in our room, Jim Warner, who taught for eighteen months with us in many subjects and not once did he repeat himself. He had attended the University of Michigan, but had gone there five years just taking courses he was interested in and enjoying it all. Philosophy, world history, medicine, and many others he taught with remarkable accuracy and insight. He made up a science-fiction movie—the characters, plot, the whole thing. It was one of the most involved plots I'd ever heard.

When there was nothing but time, day upon day, it was not impossible to put together gigantic projects under the tutelage of men who had a foreign language and could teach it. So in that time we put together language dictionaries in French, Spanish, German, and Russian. They would be taken from us by the VC on their inspection tours, but we would start over again and make them bigger and better each time.

The same was done with the Bible. We had compiled it from the one copy given to us in 1970 when treatment eased up, and we had copied everything from it. We hung onto that until an inspection lifted it again. Then we found out that, if we were last on the inspection tour, we could pass our finished products back up to the rooms already checked. By the time the guards got to us, they found nothing. If we were first in line, however, we lost everything.

That Bible became especially precious to us. In early days we tapped out Bible passages through the walls, using the code. Each man would contribute verses he knew. Sometimes we had big gaps in chapters, but we kept at it, new men coming into prison providing verses to fill out the chapters. The amount of Bible knowledge in that prison complex was surprising.

Then on Sundays, when I was asked to take over the leadership for a service, we agreed each man would take his turn sharing what he knew of the Bible. After living with the same men in prison for four or five years, you run out of new ideas, and, in order to avoid having to repeat over and over all I knew, or what the next man knew, we shared around the room. As for me, I concentrated on the history of the Old Testament, all through Kings and David, back to Genesis. We had group discussions that became a special Sunday school time. I learned more of the Bible there than I had ever gotten in my years in the church at home. It wasn't the fault of the church, but simply the difference in the environment—my eagerness here to learn, to know, to draw strength from knowledge, to pass on to others and to receive from others some amazing insights into Biblical truth. The Bible became so popular, in fact, that people were reading it all the time, even getting up at night to take their turn.

It was this fantastic pooling of knowledge in one place and the eagerness on the part of these men to learn from one another that stick out in my mind. The improvising we did for entertainment was in itself something of a major feat.

Christmas was an especially hard time on all of us from

the very beginning. At first the few of us in a room would try simply to make it worthwhile by reminding each other of the meaning of it. But thoughts of family were strong then, and the empty, heavy feeling of loneliness would hang hard. Of course, the North Vietnamese had their propaganda room where we had to go on Christmas; there they had gifts for us, and coffee and tea along with a talk with the camp commander. But even this was distorted for their own use. When we would sit down the camp commander would say, "Even though you have bombed the Vietnamese people, and even though your government murders innocent women and children, we will still allow you to celebrate Christmas."

This of course rubbed us the wrong way, and we would never take anything they offered us. We wanted nothing that was not in the daily ration, because we intended to resist their attempts to use us this way.

In later years we made our own Christmas tree—we intended to beat them out of their Christmas room by making our own. In 1970, when we had the fifty-seven men in a compound, we started planning the Christmas week early. We would shut down the Hanoi University classes, the movies, the discussions. We would plan each night of Christmas week: One night we would have a Christmas miracle story; the next night the Charles Dickens Christmas story; some nights skits were put on by various teams. And we also put together our own choir. I would deliver the Christmas message on Christmas Eve.

For our Christmas tree we would take the rice-straw mats we slept on and hang them on the wall. Then we took our olive-green socks—the VC combat socks given to us —and put them on that mat in the form of a tree. We'd decorate those socks with whitewash. On some Christmases we took pieces of paper, made ornaments out of them, and hung them in the corner of the room in the form of a Christmas tree. It wasn't much, but there was enough symbolism there to give us the spirit. And on Christmas morning at around five o'clock "Santa" would appear and we would distribute gifts. Nothing very fancy, of course. A man who didn't smoke would give his cigarettes as the gift for a man who did; the man who smoked would give candy to a third person.

I couldn't express the beauty of those Christmases, the sharing of the little things we had—a cookie, a few pieces of candy the VC had given us; and to see each man's eyes light up, the smile come on his face, to sense the intimate gestures, the deep meaning, the profound simplicity which made it so beautiful. I don't know of any other Christmases that have meant more to me.

Every Christmas Eve we were interrupted by the Vietnamese, who insisted on playing their propaganda tapes to us. They also gave us little packages of fresh fruit in a grand gesture. The Protestants would get one package, the Catholics another package. On some occasions the Protestant package was better—an orange—while the Catholics only got a tangerine. Then the Catholics might get four cookies, perhaps, and the Protestants three. The VC would come into the room, you stated your denomination—and then you got your goodies. They tried to divide us this way. But their propaganda tape was especially a spoiler for our Christmas in the room—the voice screaming about Yankee imperialism —and this was deliberately designed to throw cold water on our Christmas and remind us again of who and where we were. Sometimes they'd play an Eddie Fisher record or one by Nancy Sinatra, digging us a little more.

Once that tape was over, however, we would all move around the room and wish Merry Christmas to each other and to each man's family. And we would pound out the same message through our walls to others in the complex, and it was a moment of great feeling, of emotion, of being knitted together in something so binding to us all. It was something that welded us together, that kept us from turning on each other, that made us aware of our heritage, our faith, our beliefs, and rekindled in all of us new hope.

It was the ingenuity of these men that stood out—bent, bowed, tortured, tired, often depressed, still suffering medical problems, still suffering from lack of food, undernourished, bitten over and over by mosquitoes, and constantly harassed by the Vietnamese guards who poked and jabbed and threatened. It was their will to work, to beat the system, to hang onto something that made them what they were: Americans, people, not just military men or flyers. It was this tenacity of spirit, this desire to make mind, body, and soul stand and fight and hold on that I saw as unique and beautiful in that prison.

In all that time, on into 1970 and the late fall of that year, I had never fully recovered from my wounds received in torture either. I still sweated when I heard the key in the lock, still feared being called up again for the quiz, the ropes, the leg irons. I lay tense at times, waiting. And I prayed often that it would not come again, that the change in treatment meant we were getting closer to the end of our time. More and more I was thinking of home and family as the nights seemed longer, the days dragged, and it seemed it would never end.

And then, on November 21, 1970, the Son Tay commando raid took place, and American forces made an attempt to rescue us. Immediately security clamped down. We were moved out from Camp Faith to the Hanoi Hilton complex again, which meant the "model prison" times at Camp Faith were finished. Now they put fifty-seven people into one large room with about a twenty-one-inch-wide space per man. This was a frightening situation: With so many men jammed in together, the discipline problems were bound to get worse, and anything could happen. But the Vietnamese suspected that we had some kind of intelligence system that accounted for the Son Tay raid, that we had some outside line to our military in the south. By herding us together they could control us better and cut down any possible communication with the outside.

Moving over to the Little Vegas room in the Hanoi Complex that November, we still were optimistic about the Son Tay raid. We knew now that the American military and government were serious about getting us out. Up to now, the Hanoi radio had discouraged our belief in any such attempts in their propaganda, and we were beginning to believe by then that perhaps we would be left here forever.

In that Christmas week of 1970, jammed into the Little Vegas, tempers began to flare because we were on top of each other so much. The Vietnamese too, were becoming nervous, and they staged a big inspection to find any evidence of our communication. In that inspection they took all we had, all our extra food or clothing, but we managed to hold out and keep our Christmas tree. They talked a long time about whether to pull that makeshift tree out, but in the end decided against doing so—maybe because they weren't sure what we would do if they did.

But moral victories like that were important, small though they might seem. I remember, just before that big inspection, writing out a poem I had learned on dry cigarette-package paper. The poem was called "High Flight," and it expressed fully what an airman feels. When I knew the inspection was coming, I rolled that paper up into a small ball, and hid it in a crack in the wall. The inspectors missed it. I took it out after they went, and the words took on new meaning again. But having saved something like that, having kept it out of Vietnamese hands, made it seem a good omen. These were small things, but in our environment, in our endless days of hoping against hope, we had to have these incidents to help us resist succumbing.

I was moved again on December 30 into a room of forty-four people comprised of those who were suffering medical problems and those who were considered the troublemakers. Since I was still recovering from my torture, I was put in with them. It was good to meet new people again, of course, but the VC had put us together so they could keep any trouble down. Once again, it was our intent to beat that system, to outwit them at it, so we pulled off a New Year's party that same night. We began to chant, "This is Room Number Six, Number Six, this is Room Number Six; where the hell is Room Number Five?" This chant got louder, and other rooms began to pick it up and chant it back in loud, raucous voices. By then the VC were frightened—they thought we were getting ready to riot—so they put a stop to such parties. Maybe the New Year's party wasn't worth it then, but nevertheless we had won another bit of morale for ourselves in daring to defy the system.

Besides, we now knew we had a tool in our hands, and one the VC gave us. We knew that by a united chorus of protest on any given point we could push the camp commanders to the point of acquiescing to our demands. This was something we felt we had to have, because the more we could push them to yield for us in their face-saving, the more we gained in our own spirit.

One of the things the camp commanders would not give in to, however, was our insistence on having our own church service. We demanded an audience with the camp commander on this, but we never got it. So we took to singing for two and a half days at the tops of our voices—songs such as *God Bless America, Onward, Christian Soldiers, The Battle Hymn of the Republic,* and so on. At night we would keep singing from under our mosquito nets so they couldn't blame it on any one person.

After those two and a half days, sixty of our men were taken out and put into solitary confinement. We did, however, win a point: We were allowed to have a fifteen-minute service, which was often interrupted if we were too loud.

The point in all of it, of course, was that we were prepared now to go to extreme ends to get from the camp commanders what we believed we should have as only right and fair. We knew the risk in making our case by whatever means we had, which was sometimes no more than prolonged periods of singing. We thought, though, that the risk was worth it in terms of winning our case, no matter how small that victory might be.

Now that we had our church service without that usual Vietnamese preacher shouting his anti-imperialist slogans, the VC decided that such groups could not meet without their approval. They insisted that we write out our entire worship service—even the sermon. Well, this grated on us, and we decided we were not going to accede. So they took Commander Ned Shuman out for interrogation to force him to write out that service. We all agreed that if the VC took anyone out for isolation we would protest it by saying the Lord's Prayer in unison. This was our nonviolent way of resisting, which gave the VC no cause to make serious reprisal.

When Ned went out, we began to say the Lord's Prayer together. I wasn't sure it was a proper thing—using a sacred prayer as a weapon—because it seemed rather irreverent. Well, we went ahead anyway, and when they came and got the next man for interrogation, Commander Ed Martin, who was one of my closest friends, our praying got louder. Next was Commander Colie Haines. By the time they got to the fourth man, Commander Ted Kopfman, it was now a rumbling sound, a rising pitch of voices, and the VC were getting nervous again. They stopped taking men out, but they locked the four men they had taken into the Heartbreak Hotel in a small seven-by-seven room, and Ned Shuman was put in irons. At that, the men in our room became very resentful and wanted to storm the walls to get those men back; the junior men kept coming to me, asking me to do something. I asked them what constructive action they had in mind—and some suggested that we grab a guard and hold him hostage or, if nothing else, that we refuse to obey any more orders from the VC until those men were back.

The situation was growing uglier, and if it kept building something tragic was going to happen. One thing the VC feared was our lines of authority, our organization on rank, to gain back any kind of identity as military. We therefore agreed to make our rooms into a tight, military command program, like a Navy ship. So we organized, with a duty officer and a chain of command. Every time a VC guard came in he had to go through the chain of command to the top man in the room; the process was unnerving to them, and they did not know how to handle it.

The second thing we decided to do was carry out a stare program. During the wash period outside, we put men in strategic positions in the yard to do nothing but stare intently at the guard. We had three guards in the yard, and every day we put men out there on stare duty. Our men stared for five minutes steadily with evil-looking eyes at a guard. The guards obviously began to feel the effects of this and began to look uncomfortable. Finally the guards left the courtyard—it was too much for them. When they locked us up that night, they did not even take a head count.

As a result of this stare program, we were given our audience with the camp commander. We requested that our men be brought back, that we have better food, better medical attention, at least in accordance with the rules of the Geneva Convention. We wanted help for our asthma cases, because they were in agony trying to breathe; and their condition was hard on the rest of us, because we didn't know how to help them. We had men yet with open wounds, some who had had them for five years, wounds still draining, some of them going worse.

Well, one night the VC responded by marching into the room, maybe twenty of them, armed to the hilt. They started calling out men's names, nineteen in all, and took these men to a camp north of us called "Skid Row." It was a punishment camp. These nineteen men were in the stare program, so we had not gained much in our attempt at protest.

On March 17, 1970, we got another jab. This time the commander called The Bug, who boasted that he had tortured every American prisoner, began to put the screws on us. He had a little quiz room of his own we called The Bughouse. When we went in to him, we had to contend, not only with his savage disposition, but with that awful distraction of watching his right eye roll up into his head unexpectedly. When that happened, all that was left was the white of the eye —which was why we called him The Bug, because that rolling eye resembled that of a bug.

Well, he came strutting in one night, divided the big room

again, and put a junior officer in charge. This wrecked our command, which was built on senior officers. They knew it would, and their purpose was to destroy our organization that created unity in protest. Then they tried to get us to stand up in muster, but we refused to stand for an enlisted VC guard who was not an officer. The Bug was furious. He would not give us anything—toilet paper, medicine, food—unless the junior officer among us, so appointed, would ask for it. But for us to let the junior officer be the chain of command would destroy our organization and constitute yielding on our part. So we went seven days without cigarettes, or any time outside, or medicine, or toilet paper. They brought food and water, but nothing else.

Then one of our men who had medical problems developed diarrhea and stomach cramps, complicated by an open wound he had carried for five years, and we couldn't let him go on without medicine. So we broke down and put the word through our junior officer, Larry Carrigan, to go after medicine. Oddly enough, he had hardly left when the medical officers came in, so we were saved from having to use our junior man. It was just another indication that the VC could be forced to yield in the end, if only we resisted long enough.

Now, however, the atmosphere in our rooms was uneasy. People wanted to push further, to increase the protest, to build resistance until we received our own demands. We had in mind the ultimate possibility that, if we resisted enough, we might—who knew?—become too much of a problem and they would either begin giving us proper treatment or maybe start releasing us.

So we began a moratorium on letter-writing. None of us would write home, and the VC had been getting a lot of mileage from the propaganda about their "humane and lenient treatment" in allowing us to write. Sometimes they even would beg us to write home. We decided we would quit writing in hopes of making them bow to our demands. The VC were upset by this, so they said they would allow one letter from home to us for every one we wrote. That meant they had been holding our mail and not delivering it to us, which only made us more angry.

After six months of our moratorium on letter-writing, we decided to break it off because of general prisoner disgruntlement. We said we would write one letter for every one they let us have from home. But it didn't work, so we went back to writing regularly. By then I had had one letter that was allowed to come through to me, back in May 1970; then I got another in June. The most I received or was allowed to receive in that year was seven; I never found out how many more they were holding. But that was the end of it. I was to receive no more letters in the balance of my two years there. To this day I don't know why they refused to give me any more mail, except I was considered one of the "bad boys" of the prison, and anything they could do to make my life more miserable was done.

In late 1971, we began to see some move toward better medical treatment. Some of our resisting and protesting was getting home to somebody at the top. We had a building established as a medical room that we named the Mayo. The VC took out our very sick people, those with asthma and bad wounds, and put them in there. There was better food and treatment over there, and this helped our morale. With the establishment of the Mayo, we believed that things were changing for the better, that maybe the pressure of a truce was coming on—and who knew but that we might be going home soon?

At any rate, they took the frailest of our sick out of our rooms and into the Mayo, choosing the people to go on the basis of weight. The lighter the weight, the more qualified you were to go into Mayo. Sometimes, though, they would give special food to a man in our room without taking him out—if he looked poorly or was down in weight, the VC might give him special rations of bananas, meat, and milk. But, again, some of the men they picked did not need that food, while a wounded man might—and if they would not take that wounded man out to Mayo, why wouldn't they give that food to him in the room? We couldn't understand this kind of thinking, and it created more anxiety, sometimes precipitating a near explosion. We therefore decided to make the senior man in charge responsible for distributing the food fairly to those in need. That helped.

We noticed now that the VC were going to extreme lengths to build up the sick into healthy specimens in case an international inspection team came around to check on conditions. The will to survive was strong now, and food was a constant problem. When the VC took out one man who was pale and weak and underweight and brought him back two months later looking fat and trim, it hit us hard; because the rest of us ate all we were given in order to survive, we did not qualify for the special treatment. The guy who was a finicky eater by habit, of course, always went down first, and he then became the object of special attention by the VC, who wanted to show us all how "humane" they were. This man would also be displayed to the antiwar delegations.

We had another man who became a special target for the food treatment. He was always weak and frail, but when he got the food he would not eat it, and this created problems. Other men would fight to get it, and again we had to jump in to save the day. He was getting bananas, milk, and chocolate, things we never received, and to watch that high-calorie stuff sit there ignored by this prisoner nearly drove us out of our minds. The VC would not allow him to share it.

Finally the VC took this man and the other very frail man, before he became plump, to another camp, where they lavished blood transfusions on them. It was a desperate move on their part not to lose one body, and it meant they were feeling the pressure of accountability on this score. But the one man who would not eat would take the food and bury it rather than eat it, and the VC would give him more, thinking he had eaten it. When he did not gain weight, however, more blood transfusions were in order; this man was actually living on blood. Later they moved both men back into the room, and I was relieved, because I was afraid they would let the weaker man, Len, die. Some men did die in camp—

at least, they disappeared and we never heard from them again.

Now we were moving into late 1971. The bombings were heavier. We began to see the B-52's coming in, and these raids were heavier than ever. This was the time Haiphong was getting it.

It was at this time that a frightening thought came to me and some of the other officers in the rooms. We had been aware for some time that our being so packed in together in the rooms gave the VC easy opportunity to control us. They could, we now realized, be keeping us together for another reason: so that when and if the commando raids came in again, the VC could shoot us all in one sweep. All they had to do was toss a few grenades into our rooms, and that would be it. Or, if they saw our contingents coming in to get us, they could move us up to the Chinese border. That would be the end of us, because nobody would know where we were.

In the spring of 1971, then, we began to put together one of the most imaginative disaster plans in a prison I know of, a plan to provide for our breakout at the right time.

9

Moving to the Countdown

AT THIS POINT IN LATE 1971 we were all caught up in the hope of being released, and therefore the pressures of the VC to keep our morale low down seemed magnified. We had taken it far too long already, and we were getting desperate. The human mind in that condition had to be occupied, heavily occupied, to prevent sheer insanity or some rash move, like trying to kill a guard.

When Commander Colie Haines came to me in Room 6 of the Hanoi Hilton that spring to talk about a disaster plan, I knew it was his way of saying we had to get our men working on this just to allow them to let off steam. Of course, the purpose ultimately was to prepare for the time when the VC would shoot us all if attempts to rescue us were at hand. We were careful not to form the disaster committee to look like another escape committee. If the VC found out about it, we would really be in for it. So none of us who had been in the Annex or the Zoo served on that committee. This one four-man committee formed other committees; it was never called an escape committee, but we all knew that it really was one, because we fully intended to save our necks as best we could if there should come the time when we knew mass assassinations were contemplated.

We had a survival committee set up to organize rations

for the trip, that 110 miles to the sea; we had a committee to study the use of the AK-47 Communist machine gun in the camp used by the guards which we would get our hands on when we went out; we had a committee to study the geography, to pick the best route out of Hanoi to where we could expect a pickup; we even had a committee to study the minority groups in Hanoi, the tribes that were not urbanized and who might cooperate with us.

The recommendations we came up with in this disaster plan were: We would board up all the windows when we knew mass assassinations were near, and we had a committee studying the situation to determine when we should do this. We would use our bed boards for that, wedging these boards between the metal bars over the windows, which would act as a shield to keep the guards from sticking their guns in and shooting. Then we had a practice run one day, showing the men how to use those boards to fight off any guards trying to get in the windows.

We had men designated to watch the courtyard at all times from the ceiling vents or the windows. If they saw the guards marshaling in the yard, they would pass the word, and we would know it was time to go into action.

We formed a dispersal plan, putting half the men in one part of the room, half in another. We planned to put bed boards over a pedestal or a bunk frame, and men in these parts of the rooms could crawl under and not get the brunt of a spraying gunfire. We had a large concrete slab in the wash area that we managed to get loose, and fourteen men could crawl under that when it was leaning against the wall and get protection as well. We formed a command post in the safest corner of the room with a senior officer and a staff to control our movements.

We had exit points established: One was through the ceiling. We had another in a weak place in the wall which we could knock out with a board. We had a first-aid committee, and we had a buddy-system committee so that two men could go out together to help each other. For a man who had wounds and could not walk, we devised a plan to help him make it out by showing two men how to carry him in the fireman's carriage grip. We put supplies in our bedrolls in certain places in the rooms. We had plans to barricade the door at the right moment too, because we had to have time to make it out through the planned exits in the wall or through the ceiling.

Meanwhile, I was moved over to Room 7, and we had to develop a disaster plan, similar to that in Room 6, so we could link up with it. The team was composed of Colie Haines, who had moved over; John Dramesi, who had gone out in 1969 and been caught and returned; Ralph Gaither; and myself.

In this plan, we went even further than we had in Room 6—we cut a hole in the front wall by the door and built a facade around it with boards so the VC couldn't tell it was there. We decided to build two or three of these facades, and it took us two to three months for each one. We also worked out a plan to jam the door lock.

We had everything built, working laboriously night and day whenever we could, watching for the guards, sometimes working in the dark. And we found that thinking about new plans, new ways to get out when we had the chance to, kept us from turning on each other. It drove us on, extending us beyond our limits at times; and time passed.

In early 1972 the VC, perhaps sensing what was going on again, moved a number of our people to a camp up by the Chinese border. We had been afraid of that all along. It was a sign that they might be getting ready to do what we feared —if not to kill us, maybe to isolate us off on that border where we could never be found.

Now our labors were intensified. We decided to try to escape before being moved or killed. Even then we had to be sure we did not attempt escape prematurely. I was afraid of anything like that, because that would mean torture all over again. So we were very careful how we communicated to each other about the disaster plan, making sure only a few knew on the inside what was up, and always making sure nobody pushed the button too soon.

I was moved again, over to Room 1, this time with Dramesi. The window positions, the door structure, everything was different there. So we started all over again to put together the disaster plan that would fit the other rooms. Now it was Colie Haynes, Dramesi, and I, Gaither having been shipped to the Chinese border.

We considered tunneling out from Room 1. We could build the tunnel to the street twelve or fourteen feet away, and be ready to go on the signal. But we decided the tunnel would take six months to complete; that seemed too long— and, anyway, what would we do with the dirt?

We decided the best project for Room 1 was to work on the lock of the door. There were no iron bars on the outside of this door, as there were on the others—a practice the VC had used since my torture when they thought I might escape. The lock on the door had a little plunger and a bolt about nine inches long, three-quarters of an inch thick. The key the guards used simply depressed that plunger. So we got a piece of wire, about ten inches long, and shaped it into a right angle. One afternoon we made a try on that lock from the inside when the yard was clear of guards. We had ten people watching for them.

The first time we tried to open the lock, it was unsuccessful. Two days later we tried it again—but no luck. Meanwhile, when we were in the courtyard for our daily exercise, John Dramesi would practice opening and closing that door, working the lock, and then used the wire to test it. Finally we succeeded, and now that we had the "key" to opening that door, we knew we could go out any time we had to.

We took to practicing getting out of the ropes with a razor blade just in case we might be tied up by the VC. In complete darkness we learned to cut the pieces of cloth we were bound with, and we learned to become very proficient at it.

I soon became aware that one man on our team was not thinking simply of a disaster plan. John Dramesi, who had tried the escape in 1969 which resulted in torture for so many of us, was always thinking of a way to get out. I admired John for always seeking to fulfill the military code of taking every means to escape. The risks he took to try to break out were acts of courage in themselves. And yet we had learned in 1969 that there was no way to go out without outside help. The only way we would do it again was when we were sure we had no alternative, that the VC maybe were coming to exterminate us.

But Dramesi, nevertheless, was going to try it again. At any rate, whether he did or not, for John, like the rest of us, working on the disaster plan at least appeased his desire to escape—a kind of mental masturbation. Well, we hid the key to the lock in the wall just to make sure nobody got it, especially the VC. But in the meantime I became aware of Dramesi's movements—I knew he was shaping up an escape attempt. He was making coolie hats of bamboo sticks, using dry straw matting to shape them up; making a shirt into a pair of coolie pants, hoarding supplies in little bags. Nobody said anything to him about it, but I watched him; I wasn't about to be put through torture again for another one of his attempts to break out. We informed the senior man, Commander Bob Schweitzer. Schweitzer was told that Dramesi was going to try to go out on his own, and he laid down the law: "No escapes." Unless we went out together at the right time, we were not likely to be successful.

One morning in September 1972, I saw Dramesi going up in the ceiling. I saw the key to the lock in his hand. At that point there was nothing I could do but watch him, knowing now that what he was about to do was going to open another horrible chapter in human suffering at the hands of the VC.

But God was watching. At the very point when Dramesi was trying to work out, the VC came with an order to move us out. I couldn't believe it. At that precise moment, when Dramesi was one eyelash from making the attempt, the VC had showed up and knocked a hole in it! With moving us around, the whole cadence of the escape was thrown off.

Dramesi could not risk it then. I could only thank God, because it would have been a disaster if he had, and everybody knew it.

In late 1972, after having been moved to several different rooms in the compound, I became aware that the disaster plan had occupied almost a year of our time. That year had gone faster because of our preoccupation with outwitting the enemy, and, though we were not to use that plan, what it did for our morale was tremendous.

Now the B-52's were coming over regularly, and the shoot-downs, we noticed, were young kids. Looking at them made us realize how much time had gone by for us; it seemed like a totally new war. These kids were healthier-looking than we had been, carried a lot of weight, and had none of the ravages of torture the rest of us had when we came in.

It was good to see them, and they passed a lot of information on the war to us. We found out about POW bracelets; we found out about the long hair being sported at home, the doubleknit clothes, Richard Burton's giving Liz Taylor an enormous diamond. We heard about the miniskirts the girls were wearing, and some of the men were afraid they wouldn't get home in time to see them.

Now the camp area was changing too. The VC put on their beautification act again. More architectural imagination was going into the walls; our rooms were being spruced up. We felt that, when peace came, there would be probably an international inspection team, so we believed peace was on its way. And medical treatment began to pick up as well. We got the most complete physical we had ever had. They brought around books and even a pen and paper for each man.

One day in late October we heard a tape the VC put on over the "box" telling about the Peace Agreements, and we became very excited then. But the talks had fallen through—and they saved that for the last bit on the tape. We were left hanging again. Yet we held onto one last hope

—that maybe the VC were trying to discourage us about the talks. We felt the VC had "trial ballooned" us to see how we would take it.

Then interrogations began. The senior men were taken up and questioned about their reactions to peace. That was in November. I went up on November 4 for the quiz, the first I had had in three years. And Sweetpea was there and Spot, the camp commander. Spot asked me how my health was. I was wary now, knowing how they always began their torture in that polite manner.

"How are your arms?" Spot asked, because he had not been involved in the 1969 torture period but had probably seen the records. My arm that had been broken was still hanging out at an angle of 20 degrees from my body. I showed him my arm and told him my ear was still draining and I could not hear much through it.

Satisfied, he shifted the focus and asked me about the news, the peace talks and the peace agreement. I told him that I could not express an opinion—that he had to see Major Jim Kasler, my senior officer, who was an ace in Korea and whom the VC worked on because of his fame. He was a man I admired for his courage. Spot went on to say that we could be outside more, but we had to control each other more. I told him that, if we had the senior officers out with us, it could be done. I wanted men like Colonel Risner, Colonel Flynn, Captain Stockdale, and Captain Jerry Denton to be out with us, because we could maintain discipline among the men outside much better.

Well, we did get to go outside more. We had volleyball and basketball now, and we could see the faces of men we had talked to but never seen. Later our time dwindled back again to three hours a day, and we reasoned the bombing down south must be hot and heavy now. Whenever the bombing bothered them, they took it out on us. We were tangible; the bombers were not. But there was no bombing here in the North, with the peace agreements on.

On the night of December 18, 1972, however, the air raid siren blared. We all thought it was just a practice alert. But we could see through the windows off in the distance; it was a raid, all right. This time the B-52's were coming in heavy; it was awesome, and in a way exhilarating, because we had no way to fight where we were, but to see the planes do it for us lifted us. And for the next ten days we experienced the heaviest bombing of the war. We slept little during those raids; the city rocked under the beating. The VC began to dig deeper into their foxholes, and finally Hanoi began to evacuate nonessential personnel.

Then the guards moved their quarters closer to us; they thought the bombers would not hit the camps. Though they dug in deep to keep their hides protected, we had only our beds to crawl under. But at least we had our disaster plan there, and if the camp were bombed, we would make the best of it under the boards and the cover we had arranged.

On Christmas Eve, the last raid came and went. It was 7:00 P.M. The camp commander, Spot, came in and told us that this Christmas would not be very good for us because of the bombing. But we improvised again, sharing our little gifts, planning our skits, and making a Christmas tree.

It was past midnight on Christmas Day when the bombers came again, and we climbed up into the windows to watch, risking getting hit just to be able to identify with our planes doing their job. On the twenty-seventh they bombed quite close to our camp, and the VC told the world press that our planes had killed some of our men. But they only came close, and it would have had to be pinpoint control bombing to hit any of us. In fact, my room actually moved a few inches in one very close, solid explosion.

Well, the bombing must have had quite an effect. When it finally stopped, in the days that followed we noticed that our food was poor, which meant that their supplies had been hit hard and they had little to give to us. Another sign was that the rats were beginning to show up in great numbers again. The pickings downtown were not so good, now, and they went through our rooms at night thoroughly. We had some of our cereal bars left over and we put them in our socks at night and hung the socks on a wire which stretched from one end of the room to the other. Then we hung the sock down on a string from that wire, so the rats would have quite a time. But they managed somehow to make it across that wire and hang on it to reach down into the sock. They were desperate rats to do that, and we knew that the bombing had been devastating even to them.

But now there was no bombing. Something had happened. None of us dared to say much about it, but there was an eerie silence over everything. On January 27 peace agreements had been signed in Paris, but we didn't know. All we had was our disaster plan ready to go; we were at the windows watching for the sign that the guards were coming to do us in. Anxiety was strong in those hours. Men who had given up ever getting out were feeling it the most; some of these men had been in prison since 1965. They had lost hope somewhat, but now they refused to entertain any hope for fear of being disappointed again.

On February 2, the camp commander, Spot, came in and said, "How are you today?" It was unusual for him to come to our room, so we asked if there had been any progress in Paris. He said, "No," and we knew then something had happened for good. We always understood the reverse of what he said. Sometimes it worked, sometimes not—but we had already received some indication of peace from the guards, who could not keep a secret. A couple of them had leaked it to us when the bombing stopped: They went around with the thumbs-up sign, a gesture they'd picked up from us, indicating that something good was about to happen.

Something else was signalling the end of the war. There was a 200-foot weather tower we could see from our rooms which had been built by the Russians. The tower had lights on it to aid planes in their navigation. When the bombing started, however, those lights went out so our planes couldn't use it to home in on. We reasoned that, when those lights came on again, the war was about over. They stayed off even after the bombing—and then came on suddenly one night. It was, we knew, a good omen.

Sure enough, that next afternoon we were called out into

the middle of the camp, some 250 of us, and there the peace agreement was read to us. We were told also that we would be released in four increments according to shoot-down date.

The news was now official. We had been anticipating it for some time, of course, but the reality of it never got through to us at first. We still had a tendency to disbelieve the VC after years of being lured with false promises. But going to bed that night was different from any of the long nights behind me. Sleep did not come easily. The realization that we were about to end this long nightmare was more than we could absorb.

Well, the first group of 115 prisoners mustered in ranks in the compound. They had on their special VC issue blue shirts and pants and gray jackets. They looked trim, some of them a little bedraggled in their gauntness, some still with their scars. As they marched out the gate, I felt a longing, deep within, to be with them, still not sure we were all going to go. Yet 115 had gone out; we would surely be going now, there was no question about it.

But once they were gone, we were left, the rest of us, with a lonely feeling. A big part of us had disappeared. To wait was going to be a kind of torture for us too. We knew how uncertain the moves of the Vietnamese were, even at the best of times. I kept thinking of those men marching out to the airport, getting on that plane, cheering as they lifted off for Manila. For the rest of us remaining, who had spent so much time in this place, trying to keep hope alive, being so close to leaving now made us even more anxious.

We knew we couldn't just stand around, though. There were forty men in my room then, and on that Sunday I prepared to lead church services as usual. But instead of simply having the services in my room with the forty, we decided to have it as an entire group, disregarding the VC rule on that. On this Sunday, we thanked God for simply having survived; it was a very moving service. There were only 110 POWs left in that camp, and there wasn't a man in the room who was not conscious of those who were absent, those who had gone on home to freedom and life. And yet, looking into those faces I had come to know so well, I saw genuine expressions of peace as they all worshiped God that day for what He had done.

We were scheduled to leave the following Tuesday. Ten minutes prior to the release—and we had our new issue of clothes on by then—Colonel Norman Gaddis, the senior officer, went up for interrogation. We thought it was strange at this point; but I remembered that Colonel Robbie Risner had gone up for the same interrogation when he led his group out on the twelfth, so we expected Gaddis to come back and say, "Okay, we're free to go."

When he came back, however, he said, "Well, I've got bad news." And his face showed it. We would not be released. Gaddis added that the North Vietnamese had charged the United States with violating the peace agreements in the South.

There is no way to express what we felt then. Most of us in the group had already been in this prison complex more than six years, and this could mean another long stretch while they ironed out the details. Knowing how we all felt, Colonel Gaddis came up to me afterward and said, "I guess you should plan another church service, Red."

"Yes, sir," I said, even though it was difficult to go back and take up the routine as usual. But, again, I had to grab on to the hope that had burned in me since my shoot-down and which God never let die in me. I sat down and prepared my sermon for the coming Sunday. After giving one on worship and the joy of deliverance, what was there to say now?

I spent many hours wrestling with that—what to say, what could possibly be said. So I decided then on the book of Job. Job had had his days of trial too, maybe even more severe than ours, and he had held out, refusing to bend. I felt it was the only text to use, to prevent our becoming bitter now, to realize that God was mindful of what was going on and He would not forget.

So on the next Sunday we gathered, and just before the service God sent down His big package—one of the many He had given me these six years. We were told that we would be released that day. Colonel Gaddis said, "Let's finish the service when we get to the Philippines!"

We were put on the bus then—and, if we had any doubts about the reality of the Vietnamese release, they were dispelled when we saw the thousands of civilians outside watching us as we left. I thought of that time after shoot-down when civilians spat on me in that open grave in the ground, of those little farmers who had marched me along at the end of their homemade guns. I thought of all they had done to inflict on me the severest punishment, and yet I felt no hatred for them. They were not the "enemy" to me at all. They were people, part of the human condition, striving in their own way to arrive at some semblance of existence that would give to them a measure of happiness. I had seen them, as I did now, as a people with dedication, their own will to win and to find life, and I respected them for that. And I felt something else too, something Christ had given to me in the high point of the torture: compassion. I saw those faces as we passed by, empty faces, somber faces, faces that showed the grime and grit of everyday existence. And I wished at that point that I could share what I had of God, that they, too, in their hour of darkness would know the same presence of the Lord as I had.

Behind me, fading away into the past, were those buildings: the Hanoi Hilton, Little Vegas, Heartbreak Hotel, Zoo, Zoo Annex . . . and with them the faces of Jawbone, Sweetpea, World's Tallest Gook, Rabbit, Slug, and B. O. Plenty—still, for all I knew, fishing in Lake Fester. I saw it dissolve behind me, but the smells and sights and sounds would remain a long time, I knew.

I saw a familiar C-141 aircraft waiting for us on the field. At that moment, something broke inside me and the tears came easily. Somehow I had managed to restrict my tears to those rare times, in the nights under my mosquito net, when Hanoi Radio had gotten to me and I was down. But here, seeing that airplane waiting, I just let go, because I suddenly realized that my country had not let me down. And that great Scripture came to me, the Lord's words: "I will never leave thee nor forsake thee." Even as God had stayed at my side through all that time and taught me the things that were to change my life completely about His reality and His presence in suffering, somehow that American plane socked home some of the things that made America and God great.

Before I boarded the plane, I turned and looked at Spot, the camp commander who was now officially releasing us to our country. I remembered all those threats in prison:

"You will be here until the cows come home!"

"We will control you even when you get back to the United States!"

"You will never go home! You will be forty years old before you get home!"

But looking at Spot now, I did not feel like gloating. His face, as usual, was expressionless. For me, it was going home to a new life, to loved ones. What was it for him? I didn't know. Looking at him now, I did not think of the many hours of interrogation under him, the torture, the harassment. He was just another man in another part of the world who had done his job. Maybe he felt our going home made him lose face, since he had not broken us as he was supposed to do. But I did not see him as an animal, void of emotion. I saw him now as just a human being, and somehow I wished we could all sit down there on that tarmac and talk over what life is all about—what it could mean, free of bars and cells and all of the strange, terrifying things that go into political doctrines that separate us.

Looking at him like that, I knew I had come a long way from my first terrifying moment in that shoot-down. I had come six years in time; but in it, God had turned me around 360 degrees, so that I could stand there and look into the face of a man who had done all he could to break me and yet feel only a desire to share with him the inner, deeper secrets of God and His love and His never-ending care.

And then his face was gone. I was on that airplane, and pandemonium broke loose. As those wheels lifted off, the cheers shook the plane. And when the plane crossed over water on the way south, we all shouted, "Feet wet!"—we were no longer over North Vietnam. Those mouths opened in a wild cheer—some with teeth missing, some with faces showing physical and emotional scars, some who cried while they cheered.

No matter what anyone would say in the future about Vietnam, somehow we had won a little piece of something that no man would take away from us.

The reception at Clark Air Force Base in the Philippines was moving. We marched down the ramp of the plane and saluted and shook hands with the welcoming committee there to receive us. Behind the fences were the crowds. Maybe crowds could be bought, but certainly not the feelings they communicated to us. The spectacle was awesome. The press was there too, but we could say nothing about our torture lest it have an effect on those still left behind us. But the press continued to ask, "Do you feel any bitterness toward your country for allowing this to happen to you?"

It was an odd question to face after all the years we'd been in prison, tasting now the first breath of freedom. But I could understand in part why it was asked—it came out of the conflict the American people had over the war, the uncertainty as to whether the military men like us had been driven against our will to engage in such an unpopular war. And yet, with my six years in an enemy prison, I couldn't think of bitterness or the rightness or wrongness of a war that had put me there. I could think of names like Metzger, Sterling, Austin ... of Runyan, Van Loan, J. J. Connell, Purcell, Fleenor . . . of Martin, Kasler, Denton, Risner, Stockdale, Guarino, Sullivan ... and so many more ... and remembering them did not bring bitterness. I saw men who cared for each other, nursed each other, took risks for each other, gave up their food for each other, and devised ways to keep hope alive in each other. I could only remember men whom I had been bound to by blood; men whose wounds I had swabbed; men who had fed me, washed me, shaved me; men who became locked with my spirit; men whose hands I held onto in our mutual pain. Six years could heap a lot of bitterness on someone for the loss of all that time, but all I could remember was the human dimension, which rose to glorious heights. And God. How could I ever look back at those years in bitterness for what Christ had done for me in suffering?

No, I had no bitterness at all. So I simply told them that. Maybe it surprised some of the press—maybe it even disappointed some. But I didn't know how to explain that when a man finds God in the deepest point of darkness and comes out not even bitter at the enemy, the question hardly fits.

But from there it was home. And in seventy-two hours, March 7, 1973, it was Portsmouth, and from there to my family. For how many nights had I visualized this moment? For how many nights, throwing that little ball of bandages up and down in my cell, did I see this scene, live it over and over in anticipation? And now there it was. I was within the embrace of my wife—she who had held onto her faith for so long, who had spent so many hours with other POW wives to help free us. And my children—now grown, bigger than I could imagine, and yet, in our holding to each other, the flesh and blood could not be denied. There was Mike, blond as ever, the same blue eyes, almost on a level with mine now, his apprehension showing in his grin, now fifteen years old, only eight when I left him . . . almost a man, having shouldered the responsibilities as man of my house during those long six years. And David, now thirteen, holding tightly to my hand, not yet in that rapid growth spurt, so there were things we could do together to find the childhood that I had missed in him. And Leslie, my baby daughter, now a young lady at eleven, a little shy, holding back, making me wonder if I were a total stranger to her after all . . . and yet knowing in that shyness, that touch too that said it all, a touch of wonder maybe of who I was but the touch that, again, could not deny what was forever deeply embedded in our hearts. These were the flowers in the dried-up field of prison, this priceless treasure that I always knew inwardly nothing could ever spoil, no matter how long we were apart. I drank in the sweetness of them, the wonder of them, and I knew how important it had been to keep the vision of them alive in those long, endless nights—and it came to me how, in the same way, they had kept my face in their dreams, refusing to let time and circumstance destroy the bridge upon which we now met. I remembered Thomas Wolfe's saying, "You can't go home again," but I had come home. Home was there, unmarred, unsullied, rich in its purity and love. All the hell of six years could not destroy the bonds that held us together; all the strains of our absence, all the uncertainties of our reunion; all the black hours of a hope that flamed up so feebly, only to tell us to stand strong—now those things were all gone, and we had the sweet reality of faith rewarded, of enduring love fulfilled.

With all these emotions rising to a peak in so short a time, I was still to face that big moment in Alanton, a suburb of Virginia Beach, my home, when I looked into the faces of over five hundred friends and neighbors who had come to welcome me back. Again, there was no way to express what I felt in that welcome. As I looked at them crowding around in the yard, I realized that those nights in Vietnam when I thought nobody cared—that it was too much for them to care with all their own problems, that they really had no obligation to care—were all finally dispelled. At that moment I knew the bonds of the human spirit, the capacity of people to reach out, to share the agonies as willingly as the triumphs.

And then I turned to my home. Oddly, when I walked into that house with my family, when I looked at the walls and pictures, as I gazed upon every area that I had seen in my dreams in those long nights of darkness, the trees, the yard, every inch—I suddenly was too overwhelmed to absorb it.

But I was here now.

Yes, it would take time to adjust, not only for me, but for my family. There would be times I would wake up and hear the key rattling in the lock, and my stomach would knot up in anticipation of more torture. There would be times I would see the whole prison again as clearly as when I woke up in those damp, chilly mornings in the jungle and looked out through the peephole in the door.

But I *was* home, and Christ had brought it all together. All my doubts, my weak faith, my imperfect knowledge of His ways were put aside in the wonder and the reality of this moment. And now I knew the why of the suffering. Now I sensed the purpose of my own Gethsemane there in Hanoi— I had to be humbled before I could know the perfection Christ had in mind for me. I knew now that there was an honor in the very character of Christ that I had not possessed while my world was running on its usual noncrisis routine. As *Proverbs* 18:12 puts it, "before honor is humility"; I knew now exactly the strange, mysterious power of that message, and the scars that I would carry the rest of my life would testify to it. Before I could attain the mountaintop, I knew that I must go through the valley. Maybe this isn't true of everyone who knows Christ, but He knew what I had to go through to enter fully into the knowledge of Him and then to experience the absolute joy of freedom and reunion with my loved ones. I knew now that every experience I had in prison was contributing to my journey through the valley—but in those experiences He was trying to prove to me that He had not forsaken me. I did not see it all clearly then; now, however, I knew that it had not been accidental, that it was not something the Vietnamese controlled in the end, but that God shaped and designed every moment, that I might come to a more perfect man in Him.

Whatever honor I had carried into Vietnam, then, as an American, a military man, the achievements of my past life were nothing compared to what I now sensed in what He had given to me of His character, His knowledge. I had been broken in that prison, brought to the very end of myself, allowed to suffer so I might know how to help those who would suffer around me. I had gone to Vietnam a respected churchman who had a healthy, ideal family—but had not the inner capacity, in God or anyone else, to minister genuinely to the suffering of another person. For some reason, known only to the Lord, I had been chosen of Him to be that instrument for Him, and what I had gone through would bring a new sensitivity to the needs of others and perhaps an example of the goodness of God to them. Through my suffering, others could see proof that He would keep them in their hour of darkness as well.

The honor I know now, then, is not mine. It is all of God. The honor is not in terms of winning anything in Vietnam so much as it is in attaining an entirely new dimension of what counts in God's eyes in terms of understanding the totality of man, myself, and those around me. My human energy and will went as far as it could, but in the end it was God and God alone who made the difference, who widened the margins of life in His own miraculous way, who took my broken, weak body and soul and put them back together again.

Looking back on it now, I am grateful too that God gave me insight into the levels of courage in the midst of suffering. I wish I could have been braver for my roommates in that prison. I still sense the many hours of real fear that all of us experienced in those long years. Yet, in that fear, I felt that Christ was able to do more in me than if I had counted only on my strength and courage. At the same time, however, I was also allowed the privilege of witnessing bravery in others. I know now that the brave man is not the man with ice water in his veins; he is, rather, the one who is afraid but still does the job. Kelly Patterson, among many others, was that kind of man. Thinking of Kelly, I still feel the pain of losing him. He knew what it would cost him going on that eighty-first mission even as I; yet he went, risking all, to do what he knew he had to do. I wish now, as I will often do in the future, that Kelly could have lived and come to know the Lord as I did in the darkness of that prison. I cannot fathom why I was chosen to go through it and live, and he should die. That knowledge I must leave to God. But I thank Him too that I was allowed to see bravery in men like Kelly, which is apart from the military hero image, but that which goes with men who are men. There is an honor they keep in their death, and I know I shall always revere it in them.

When I look at my wife in our home, I trace every line of her face, which I had seen so often in those dark hours past. And I know now what her faith meant to me in those long months and years too. She had given me the seed of my faith back in college; she had cultivated it carefully and lovingly through the years. Neither she nor I realized that that faith, so fragile a thing when I flew that last mission, was to become the vital factor to my survival. Now I knew with overwhelming awareness that in my wife—who waited for me, prayed for me, and never lost her assurance in my return—I had someone who was indeed as precious a gift of God to me as life itself. Such faith and love is the rock that the Scriptures talk about, and now I knew what it meant.

I knew again in this moment of reunion with her what that verse really meant: "For all things work together for good to them that love God" (*Romans* 8:28).

But, even more than that, I knew now what the apostle Paul meant when he said, "Who shall separate us from the love of Christ? Shall tribulation, or distress, or persecution, or famine, or nakedness, or peril, or sword?" These things are very real to me now. And Paul answers, "For I am persuaded that neither death, nor life, nor angels, nor principalities, nor powers, nor things present, nor things to come, nor height, nor depth, nor any other creature, shall be able to separate us from the love of God, which is in Christ Jesus our Lord" (*Romans* 8:35, 38–39).

The darkness of loneliness and pain was worth it all to enter into the knowledge of that fantastic truth.

Epilogue

THE LAST SERMON I had prepared as prison chaplain in Hanoi was constructed out of the gloom and despair I felt about never being released. Strangely, even mysteriously, God took me to the *Book of Job*, to the story of a man who had had his share of trials and recovered. I put together a sermon from that book, but I never did deliver it, because the North Vietnamese released us just before the Sunday service. Instead, we decided to hold that service in Clark Air Force Base in the Philippines after we landed.

The words I prepared, under the inspiration of God's Spirit while in captivity, took on new meaning and perhaps even more pertinence when I spoke them in freedom. This is the part of the sermon that stands out for me even now; I still think of it whenever I am tempted to ask the reason for what I endured:

Job was a perfect, righteous and upright man who had great wealth, more than any other man in the land. He had seven sons and three daughters. He was a holy man and loved God, and God loved him.

But Satan was able to come in between the Lord and Job, so Job lost all his wealth, little by little. His house was blown down. He lost his seven sons, his three daughters. He was covered with boils from the bottom of his feet to the top of his head. All the people turned their backs on Job. This went on for many years.

But Job fell down on his knees and worshiped God and never once lost his integrity. During the period of years which held great suffering, he did not renounce his faith in God, but he endured all that Satan could offer; and God held him in highest esteem, and when God returned to him he made him twice as wealthy. God returned his children, his seven sons and three daughters, and gave him a long life, and he lived to be one hundred and forty years old.

God says, "My son, remember well these words I have spoken to you, for they are true and cannot be denied. As long as you live you will be subject to change whether you like it or not; now glad, now sorrowing; now pleased, now displeased; now devout, now undevout; now vigorous, now lazy; now gloomy, now merry; without labor no man can come to rest; without battle no man can come to victory, and the greater the battle the greater the victory."

We have just had our greatest battle, and thus we are just beginning to enjoy our greatest victory.

Appendix I

Some thoughts from James L. Johnson:

There are many reasons why I felt the story of Captain Eugene McDaniel should be recorded in print. First, of course, is that his story emphasizes the traits that help man to survive the worst that may happen to him. In a time in history when man seems to be so ready to succumb to the pressures of the hour, to bow to the destructive elements he cannot control and then ultimately to resign himself to "things as they are," Captain Red McDaniel, like others of his comrades, revives the dormant spirit that moves people to overcome at all costs.

Second, of course, is his own journey to spiritual maturity and his own new awareness of the miracle of Christ in his life. For the many in the faith who suffer their own midnight hour of pain and the questioning that goes with it, Red McDaniel's testimony helps to clarify some of that mystery and lends new credence to the scriptural fact that all things do, in fact, "work together for good to them that love God" (*Romans* 8:28).

Third, Red McDaniel's recounting of his story is, as he admits, his own view. What makes his story and his character significant is the testimony of those who knew him and willingly vouch for his character and courage. The following excerpts from letters received—not solicited by him—from fellow prisoners testify to his stature as a man and a Christian and provide credibility for his role in that six years of confinement. If it is true that a man's deeds and character are judged finally by his peers, then Captain McDaniel's life during his darkest hour deserves to be told and shared abroad:

". . . after hearing the stories of many of our fellow POW's, it's not hard to determine the facts from the gilded stories. . . . Red did his utmost to withhold any essential information from the enemy during the maximum torture sessions of 1969. There are certain facts of which people on the outside have no grasp—one of them is this: only a very few men have the courage, conviction and strength that it takes to continue to doggedly resist the enemy in excruciatingly painful torture over a long period of time. Red is one of the very few who can and did!"

—LARRY GUARINO, COLONEL, U.S.A.F.

". . . Commander McDaniel was most effective and aggressive in obtaining communication codes and relaying and originating important information. These acts were unusually conspicuous displays of courage and initiative in view of his relative inexperience as a POW—which often inhibited other new men who tended to be intimidated by the vicious punishment known to result from being caught in intercell communications. From this period of observation and from personal associations with him for years before and during our incarceration, I consider him to be one of the finest men I know. . . ."

—J. A. DENTON, REAR ADMIRAL, U.S.N.

". . over the years as POW, Commander McDaniel demonstrated that he would suffer brutal and barbaric torture with the very real possibility of death rather than aid the enemy or conduct himself in a manner that would be injurious to his country, his fellow men or be dishonorable. He is considered to be one of the very few truly outstanding individuals that this officer has ever encountered; superb in all respects as a man, an intensely loyal and patriotic American. . . . He is a man of strong faith and devotion to God . . . he continually demonstrated trust in that which he believed, never doubting, never wavering, only optimistically looking ahead to the future and never bemoaning the present. He is deeply religious but never overbearing in his beliefs. He frequently conducted inspirational religious services for those who desired to participate. In more than twenty-three years (Academy time included) of Naval service, I have never been associated with a single officer with whom I would rather serve, whether in the harsh realities of combat or peace, in my home or in public."

—EDWARD H. MARTIN, COMMANDER, U.S.N.

". . . it was during the early days of imprisonment, when I was trying to recover from my wounds incurred during my shoot-down, that Red McDaniel's character had a chance to blossom. Even though in rough shape himself, he picked me up off the floor and nursed me back to good health. He helped feed me, tended my wounds, held our rusty old pail while I relieved myself and would even wipe me clean. I will always be impressed by Red's solid faith, high moral standards, supreme patriotism and boundless love of family. I can't express his characteristics well enough to portray adequately the very impressive man he is."

—WILLIAM J. METZGER, LIEUTENANT COMMANDER, U.S.N.

". . . how do you describe a man who was always ready, under the most trying circumstances, to go seventy-five per cent of the way, who was always ready to buoy the feelings of any of us in a moment of depression? Who had such compassion for his fellow men that even after suffering two weeks of terrible, harsh torture he would, when saying grace before our meager meal, ask the Lord to 'bless the Vietnamese, friend and foe alike'? Describe him! Words simply will not convey the attributes held and always modestly displayed by a man who in my eyes stands ten feet tall, 'The Big Red One'!"

—JOHN VAN LOAN, COLONEL, U.S.A.F.

". . . neither the Vietnamese officers nor the guards ever befriended or warmed to any prisoner during our internment. However, for a few they developed a certain respect because they had observed their guts and unbending resistance under torture. They realized that these men would never compromise their beliefs or bow to their efforts to exploit them for propaganda purposes. It was men like Red McDaniel that they begrudgingly respected. It is men like Red who give the United States Military its proud tradition."

—James H. Kasler, Colonel, U.S.A.F.

These excerpts are only a few of the testimonies to Captain Eugene McDaniel's character under great stress. As America approaches its bicentennial celebration, I am particularly gratified and privileged to share in telling his story, which personifies that great American and Christian spirit that I pray will never die.

Appendix II

RED McDANIEL HAD NO IDEA what his wife, Dorothy, was feeling in those hours of uncertainty about whether he was alive or dead. Red's prayer that she might somehow *know* that he was a prisoner, that he was alive, was answered in a remarkable way. It was not in some heavenly vision or even "the still small voice." It was simply that Dorothy's faith, in the same mold as Red's faith, refused to allow her to believe otherwise.

Her reaction, her "adjustment" to his absence, and her determination to cling to what hope she had are recounted here in her own words.

May 19, 1967, was one of the first warm days that spring. I was on the patio, wearing an old pink-and-white-checked bathing suit, reading Red's mail, and relaxing in the knowledge that his ship was "off the line" and on the way to Cubi Point. I was always more relaxed when I didn't have to think about Red flying the missions over the North.

I heard the front doorbell and hesitated to answer it, dressed as I was. When I did answer, I saw Commander Bill Small, dressed in his "whites," signifying a special occasion; the wife of Red's commanding officer was with him.

This was frightening to me, but my thought was: "Whom have they come to tell me about? Not Red; he's in port. Then who?" (Sometimes, when a good friend was shot down, the people whose job it is to notify the wife would let you know so that you could be on hand to help out.) I invited them in. Commander Small asked me to sit down, and then he told me that Red's plane was down. Red had successfully ejected and would probably be rescued within hours. Somehow I could not hear what Commander Small was saying, and he had to repeat the message several times.

For four days I clung to the hope that Red would be rescued as the messages continued to come: "Search and rescue efforts still underway." Red was in a "safe area" and would surely be picked up. It never occurred to me that he wouldn't.

Four days later, on May 23, the casualty officer assigned me by the Navy brought me a message: "SAR [search and rescue] discontinued. Presumed captured." The word "presumed" hit me like a ton of bricks and made me furious. I fairly screamed, "How can they *presume* that? They must keep on looking for him." I had a vivid mental picture of Red in a hostile jungle, waiting for the helicopters, and I imagined how he would feel when they didn't come.

My parents, who had always been a source of great strength to me, arrived the day after Red was shot down. They had the deepest faith of anyone I knew and had taught me that "all things can be wrought by prayer." Since I first received the news about Red, I had spent the hours subconsciously counting on their appearance, confident that my dad's prayers would work a miracle and produce an angel to pick up Red, since the Jolly Green Giant was obviously incapable of doing so. This was not to be. I discovered that my dad was human and that he was hurting just like the rest of us mortals. He and Red had been very close; they had a wonderful father-son relationship, and my father could not bear the thought of Red being in trouble.

Later that year, in my own childhood bedroom, my dad

said to me through his tears, "I'm sorry I wasn't stronger when you needed me."

"You and Mother gave me what I needed for this moment years ago. Thank you for that," I said. I knew that, had I leaned on them, or on any other person, in May, I would still be leaning for the duration of Red's captivity. My faith to this day would still be "second-hand." Instead, the time had come for me to test the faith my parents had taught me. I had to learn to lean on my heavenly Father, not my earthly one.

Next to my almost terrifying concern for what was happening to Red, I was frightened for the children. Red and I were very conscientious parents. Both of us had been teachers and had studied child psychology and behavior. I was overwhelmed with a sense of responsibility to them—and I was afraid of what a home without a father would do to them. Yet it was this concern for them that kept me going from day to day. Every morning when I woke up, the reality would hit me in the face like a splash of cold water and I would think, "I cannot do this job without Red. They *cannot* grow up without a father." They were so young to have their mother cease to be an authority on every subject, and now I had to say, "I don't know," to their many questions.

"Where is Daddy?"

"I don't know."

"When will he come home?"

"I don't know."

"Is he dead?"

"I don't think so."

"How long will he be gone?"

"I'm not sure."

"Will he write?"

"I hope so."

"Will we ever see him again?"

I was torn between my desire to be realistic and honest with them and my desire to protect them. My heart ached for them—for all of us.

The children cried a lot. David had nightmares and would wake up in the middle of the night asking me questions like, "What kind of hats do the North Vietnamese wear?" He would create battles all over the den floor with his little two-inch plastic soldiers and his cowboys and Indians. One of them would be Red and the others were always the VC. Red always won—against overwhelming odds.

Mike tried to be grown-up, to "help Mommy be happy." A bittersweet moment was the time he asked my sister, Mary Joe, who had come to spend a few days with us, to stop at the florist, where he bought white daisies for me with his allowance money. His loyalty to Red and his attempts to take over as man of the family at the age of nine were deeply touching. I encouraged him to invite our good friend, Captain Don Ross, to go with him to the Cub Scouts' Father-Son Banquet, but he refused, saying Don was not his father and therefore couldn't go. Mike went alone, his young shoulders squared.

Leslie, barely four, was too young to realize what had happened. All she knew was that her warm, familiar world was suddenly full of turmoil, tears, and panic. Perhaps she suffered most of all, because she couldn't understand the reasons. She was bewildered. I thought she was unaware of Red's ordeal and tried to avoid the subject. I learned I was mistaken. One night when she was six she was having dinner with our good friends, Commander Hoot Foote and his wife Laura. As she watched Hoot pile food on his plate she said, "Do you always eat that much? My father never gets enough to eat." She was very much aware.

But we managed. I made a conscious effort to live one day at a time and tried not to project too far into the future, because it was a great unknown. The children and I were surrounded by many friends who were ready and willing to help. We lived in a wonderful neighborhood where there were many activities to keep us busy. Our finances were no problem. The people in our church were concerned about us. The children were doing well in school; the boys were involved in athletics. My days were busy with running the house and keeping the children relatively happy, and my fear for them gradually subsided and was replaced by thoughts of Red's ordeal. It is a terrible thing to know that the one you love is suffering and that you can't see or feel or touch him in any way. When Red came home and told me of the torture and the deprivation, none of it was any worse than the things I had envisioned.

An overriding concern was the desire, the *need*, to hear that he was alive. I started to pray just to *know* in black and white—just to have *one* letter from Hanoi. I never really thought of him as dead. I knew in my heart that he was alive. I thought, "We were so close. I'm going to know it, some way, if he dies." But I felt that it was risky to promise the children anything on only my intuition, so I *needed* to have one letter. Also, I thought, if Hanoi will acknowledge that they are holding him, they will keep him alive until the war is over; they will have to account for him. I thought of a letter as something of an insurance policy that I would lock in a safe-deposit box and use someday to tell the world that Hanoi had acknowledged holding him captive.

By late 1968 there was still no word. I was ready and willing to enter wholeheartedly into the letter-writing campaigns to Congress and the news media that Captain Jim Stockdale's wife, Sybil, and other wives had initiated. I was reluctant, as they were, to do anything public, for fear of making Red a more valuable pawn in Hanoi's hands or singling him out for special pressure or abuse.

By 1969 our campaign had grown from quiet letter-writing to public speech-making and television appearances. Many of us had become convinced that public pressure would "open Hanoi's prison doors" wide enough to get a glimpse of what was going on. We thought a public outcry might force some acknowledgments of names and allow us some mail from those men who had never written. Perhaps pressure would result in better treatment. The rationale was that Hanoi had sent out some propaganda films showing POWs receiving "humane and lenient treatment." We would call their bluff by our public denials of the "humane and lenient treatment" and use their obvious concern for world opinion to our advantage. We were still worried about how our actions would affect the men, but we felt we had to take the chance. One of the first articles written about the POWs was in the *Air Force Digest*: "The Forgotten Men of the Vietnam War." Our slogan became: "Don't let them be forgotten!" It began to appear on signs, bumper stickers, and billboards.

One of the first speeches I made was before the congregation of the First Baptist Church in Virginia Beach in October 1969. The POW wives planned a National Day of Prayer and my pastor, Dr. Waddell Waters, had been one of the driving forces in our effort to get it organized. It was his idea to get our two local Congressmen to sponsor a bill declaring a Day of Prayer. The bill was passed and the wives spoke in churches, asking for prayers for the prisoners, and passed out letter-writing suggestions. While the day fell far short of being "national," it was a beginning. And we became more and more organized.

In 1970 the National League of Families organized on a national scale, with headquarters in Washington. Each state had a coordinator to plan publicity. In late summer of 1970 I became the coordinator for Virginia (replacing Captain Jim Mulligan's wife, Louise, who had really started things moving in our area). We had an areawide petition signing. Then we sent the mayors of Virginia Beach and Norfolk, along with a newspaper editor and a student body president, to Paris to meet with the North Vietnamese. Their journey attracted a lot of fanfare and publicity throughout the world.

In March 1970, responding to the public pressure, Hanoi started to release some names and to allow some of the men to write. A partial list of names was released, and Red's name was on it! In the same day there was a solar eclipse which took up most of the front page of the local paper. Down at the bottom was an article announcing that Red McDaniel was now confirmed by Hanoi as being alive. The big news that day for Mike, David, Leslie, and me was not the solar eclipse. In fact, the sun never shone more brightly for us!

The timing of the list was important. The children were now twelve, ten, and six, and their questions about Red were becoming harder to answer. I was beginning to wonder if I was being realistic with them, clinging as we were to the knowledge we had that he had gotten out of the plane three years ago. I didn't want to make promises about the future that couldn't be kept. When they said, "When Daddy comes home—" I would say, as matter-of-factly as I could, "Well, you know, he may *not* come home." Mike and David always insisted, "He *will* come home."

In April we received the letter we needed so much and I almost wore it out reading it and rereading it. I would get up in the middle of the night and take it out just to touch it and make sure it was real. At last I could say to the children, positively, "Your father is alive!" And I could hold his letter in safekeeping as proof that he was being held by the North Vietnamese. I felt that now they would have to account for him at the end of the war and they knew it, so at least they would keep him alive.

In spite of the relief and gratitude I felt, I was afraid that my public efforts had in some way singled him out for additional pressure to make propaganda statements. I thought, What price will we have to pay for this letter? I had always been thankful that Red had not been used for Hanoi's propaganda. Knowing him and his complete dedication and loyalty to U.S. policy, I had known that if I ever saw him on film or in the press spouting Hanoi's line, it would mean he had been broken. I knew how important resistance to the enemy would be to him.

Nevertheless, the letter was an added incentive to remain involved in the POW campaigns. To me the letter was an obvious response by Hanoi to the public pressure that was building up; I believed that if we continued to hammer away the treatment of the prisoners might improve and perhaps other men would be allowed to write home.

The exposure was hard for me, personally. I hated being in the public eye and baring my soul to the world. And sometimes I felt torn. Was I so preoccupied with the POW work that I was neglecting the children? I spent a lot of time away from home. Was I singling Red out for special treatment? Was I making things worse for him or helping? Was I really accomplishing anything? How long could we sustain our efforts? I got so tired and discouraged.

By the end of 1971 I had run out of steam and had no new ideas for the publicity campaigns. I was thankful that other interested groups in the country had taken on the POW issue because I knew we could not afford to let it die down. I began to wonder if government officials in Washington were doing enough to insure the return of the men, but I was afraid to say anything in public that would sound disloyal. I was sure that anything I said in the press would be repeated over the "box" in Red's cell in Hanoi. But at the same time I was afraid that we were not saying enough. It was hard to have absolute faith in the U.S. policy as the troops were being withdrawn while the POWs remained. I was afraid strong military action might be necessary in the end, and I wasn't sure the American people would back that, even for the POWs. I hated to think it would be necessary to escalate the war again. I really wanted an "honorable peace." I thought the ultimate tragedy would be for Red and the others to come home "on their knees" and spend the rest of their lives knowing that the sacrifices they had made had been for nothing. I didn't fully understand the war, but I knew Red had believed in it when he left, and I understood the extent of his commitment and devotion to duty. At the same time, I felt the necessity to keep the POW issue alive until a settlement was reached which included their release.

By mid-1972 I had withdrawn from the POW work. I tried to say, "Lord, it is in Your hands," and mean it, but I was really afraid. I had no real sense of direction, and at times I wondered if Red would spend the rest of his life in his prison cell. As the 1972 elections approached, there were new peace initiatives, but I was afraid to get my hopes up. Just before the election Dr. Kissinger announced that "peace is at hand," but by Christmas the United States had renewed heavy bombing of the North. Perhaps I should have recognized that as the beginning of the end, but I thought, "Here we go again." I barely made it through Christmas.

It surprised me to look back and see that the time of my greatest discouragement was also the time I was becoming more involved with leading Friendship Bible Coffees, which are study groups sponsored by Christian Women's Clubs.

I was not an adequate leader, but I think the class members benefited because they knew our family's situation and could see that God was working in my life. They thought of me as nothing special, as simply one of them, searching just as they were. The difference was that my problems were bigger than most of theirs. When I realized how God was using the situation, I thought of the verses in II Corinthians 1 that tell us that Christ "comforts and strengthens us in our hardships and trials . . . so that when others are troubled . . . we can pass on this same help and comfort God has given us." I began to see that as part of the purpose God had for my sufferings. There were some things I needed to know and was beginning to understand. I realized how shallow my spiritual life—and Red's—had been, how busy we had been building our home and making a living, and I wondered if I could share all this with him in any meaningful way if and when he ever got home. It was a lack of faith on my part not to know that it was a learning time for him, too.

"Thou hast given us our hopes and dreams. We trust Thee to unfold them in time to save us from despair." Those words are from a prayer in *Windows of Heaven* by Gler Clark. I found them in August 1967, when the reality of our situation had begun to hit me. They became a sort of private prayer for me.

I was standing in a hotel lobby in 1972 after a League of

Families meeting, waiting for my ride home. I was close to despair. I knew I had gone my limit, and I had no energy left for more meetings or campaigns. Letters from Red were few. Mike was in his teens now, and his father was still away. David and Leslie would soon be teenagers, too. Years and years of our lives—years and years of Red's life—would it never end? I looked up and saw Gloria Earley, my good friend from home, and I thought, "What is she doing here?" Gloria has had a tremendous influence on my spiritual growth and had encouraged me to lead the Bible study groups. When I saw her my tears came in a flood. "Don't despair," she said. *Despair!* "We trust Thee to unfold them in time to save us from despair!" I knew then why Gloria was in the lobby of the hotel. She thought she was there to attend a Methodist Women's Conference, but I knew that *one* reason she was there was to bring God's word to me: "Don't despair."

I thought about that day, and other such times of help coming from the most unexpected sources, when I was asked to tell about my faith in the summer of 1973 after Red came home. I wondered, How do you put into a few words that gradual awareness of God's voice speaking, of God's hand working, until it becomes a sure, steady knowledge of His love? How do you explain His power to work best when we feel most helpless? Just before my part on the program the soloist sang "Through It All." I thought the words expressed my spiritual experiences far better than anything I had planned to say, and so I began my testimony: "Through it all I learned to trust. . . . I would underscore the word *learned.*" There were times when God seemed far away.

There were other times when He was very close and very real. Gradually the times He was real became sufficient to carry me through the awful hours when I did not feel his presence.

"I learned to depend upon His Word." The songwriter had the Bible in mind. Many times portions of Scriptures I had learned in my youth would come to me in the middle of the night (Psalm 91, for example), or in the middle of a speech, or during the many evenings I would sit alone on the front steps after the children were in bed. "Thy word have I hid in my heart...."

Church attendance should have been a source of great comfort, but, although I went to church regularly, it was the hardest hour of the week for me. It wasn't the church's fault. Red had been a deacon in the First Baptist Church and one of his duties was to serve as an usher on Sunday mornings. Every Sunday I would brace myself for the service, and when the ushers went forward to collect the offering I would begin to cry. It seemed so wrong and unfair that Red's tall shoulders weren't among those lined up in front of the altar. I remember once delivering an ultimatum to God: "If You want me here on Sunday mornings, as I believe You do, then turn off these tears. It's embarrassing and it upsets the children." God wasn't impressed with my ultimatum, I learned; He had something else in mind for me. I started wearing dark glasses and sitting in the balcony. But I continued to go, partly because I wanted the children to have the same foundation my parents had given me—and I continued to cry. It was the loneliest time of the week, surrounded by people who really cared about us, and it set the tone for Sundays, which were hard anyway since we had always spent Sunday afternoons doing some family activity together. A large part of my prayer became, "Please get me through Sunday."

It came to me gradually that Red had none of the traditional "spiritual helps" I had always thought necessary—the church, the Bible, a pastor. After Hanoi confirmed the fact that he was a POW, three years after his capture, I stopped envying those wives who had had definite word from the beginning—because now I could actually visualize him in a dingy cell, alone, in solitary, or being tortured. But I could also imagine the Lord ministering to him in that cell without benefit of church, Bible, or pastor. I didn't doubt God's power to do so, because I felt His presence primarily when I was alone and heard His voice in the most unlikely ways. That realization was a source of great comfort to me. I began to understand why it was part of God's glorious plan for me that His help came, not primarily through His church, not always through His servants, not even through His written Word when I would sit down purposely to read it, but directly from Him to me. "My help cometh from the *Lord*." I wanted to shout it.

The A-6 Intruder aircraft which Commander McDaniel flew on his last mission over North Vietnam. *Official U.S. Navy photo.*

A happier moment, when Commander McDaniel cuts a portion of cake celebrating the 75,000th landing aboard U.S.S. *Enterprise.* Assisting him is Lieutenant James Kelly Patterson, McDaniel's bombardier-navigator. (Patterson died on that fateful eighty-first mission after ejecting over enemy territory.) *Official U.S. Navy photo.*

Above: After more than six years in a Hanoi prison, Red McDaniel *(left)* steps to freedom at Gia Lam Airport, Hanoi, and a warm welcome from military personnel. *Official U.S. Air Force photo.*

Opposite top: The greatest moment in Red McDaniel's life was when he saw his wife, Dorothy, waiting with open arms, a reunion he had dreamed about every night for more than six years in the Hanoi prison complex. Just as eager was his daughter, Leslie, ten, who hardly remembered him but "just knew he was my daddy."

Right: "It was worth it all for this moment," Red McDaniel said as he threw his arms around his family only two days after his release from prison.

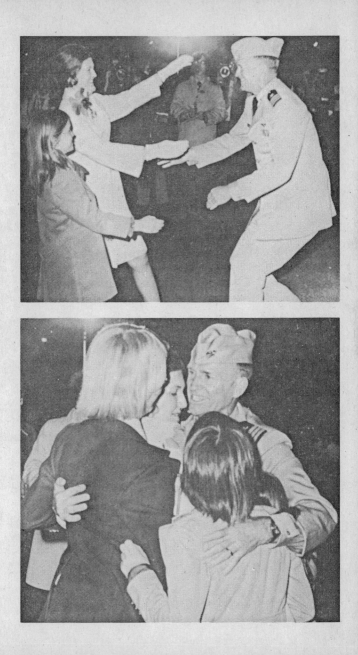

Above: "Welcome home, Red." McDaniel is greeted by a crowd of five hundred friends and neighbors upon his arrival at his home in Virginia Beach. *Official U.S. Navy photo by William J. Pointer.*

Opposite: Dorothy McDaniel never lost faith that her husband would return alive, but "sometimes it was loneliest when we as a family went to church, because there we were so conscious of his absence." *Official U.S. Navy photo.*

Right: Dorothy helped organize rallies with other wives of POWs in an effort to create pressure for better treatment and to win their release. Here she helps kick off a campaign to send a special delegation to Paris to make their case to the North Vietnamese. *Official U.S. Navy photo.*

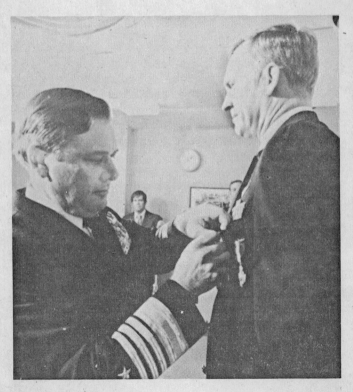

Left: Admiral James L. Holloway III, Chief of Naval Operations, pins the Navy Cross to Red McDaniel's uniform in special ceremonies in Norfolk. In addition, "for outstanding leadership and heroism during his prison experiences," McDaniel was also awarded two silver stars, three bronze stars, the Legion of Merit, and the Naval Commendation Medal.

Above: The scars remain for Red McDaniel, but "God made something new of me because of them." A new life with his family was a part of the miracle God gave him in answer to his prayer; from left: Dorothy, Mike, Leslie, and David. *McIntosh Studio.*

Next page: The eternal sea continues to stretch out for Captain Eugene McDaniel as he faces up to a new command in the Navy. "The bravery of those my comrades in that prison experience moves me on to serve my country," he says. "And now I know I don't go alone—God goes with me." *Philip Garvin.*

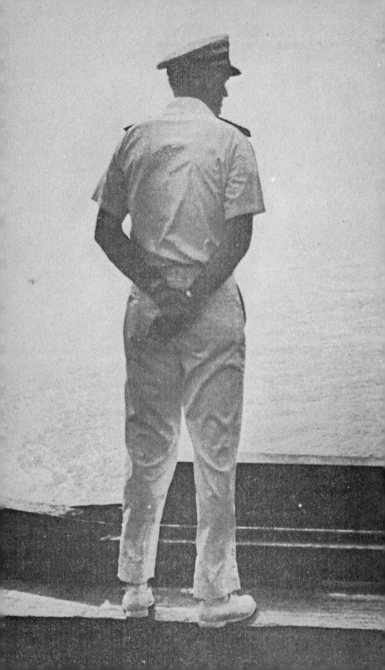

The American Defense Foundation
The American Defense Institute

Red McDaniel has survived the brutal nightmare of Vietnam, but his great joy in returning home to family and freedom is tempered by a deep and growing concern for the land he loves.

Red served his country with honor for six long years of North Vietnamese torture and imprisonment, then continued on active naval duty for nine years after his release. His 27 years of distinguished military service is not, however, the final chapter of Red's incredible dedication to his country. In 1983, he created the American Defense Foundation (ADF), a 501(c)(4) non-profit organization, as a vehicle for his patriotic convictions and strong moral principles.

ADF has earned the respect of policy-makers in Washington and across the country as a responsible advocate of strong defense policies. ADF speaks with authority on a variety of national security and defense topics.

ADF functions as a clearinghouse for defense-related information for Members of Congress, college and high school students, and the public at large. It sponsors speakers and publications, produces advertising and media programming, and provides support services to local and national branches of government.

Red McDaniel also heads the American Defense Institute (ADI), which is the educational arm of the now highly successful ADF. The Institute is a 501(c)(3) non-profit, non-partisan organization and all contributions to it are tax-deductible.

The Institute sponsors a variety of educational programs such as the National Speakers Bureau, the ADI Washington

Intern Program, the annual National Defense Fellowship, and the National Security Leadership Seminars. The Institute also conducts non-partisan, worldwide military registration drives to encourage military personnel to exercise their right to vote.

The ADF/ADI perspective stresses the value of freedom and our responsibility for protecting it with a strong national defense. Both ADF and ADI place special emphasis on young people, who are the future leaders and protectors of America. ADF and ADI believe the investment in young people is an investment in the continued security and freedom of America.

Dear Red,

I want to help you to keep America strong and free. No American should ever again experience the horrors you lived through in a communist prison.

Your effort to prepare young Americans to lead our nation in future years has my support.

I AM ENCLOSING MY TAX-DEDUCTIBLE CONTRIBUTION TO THE AMERICAN DEFENSE INSTITUTE.

$250____ $100 ____ $50 ____ $25 ____ Other _____

Name _____

Address _____

City _____ State_____ Zip _____

Please make checks payable to:

AMERICAN DEFENSE INSTITUTE
214 Massachusetts Ave., N.E.
P.O. Box 2497
Washington, D.C. 20013-2497

(202) 544-4704

The American Defense Institute is a non-profit educational organization [501(c)(3)]. All contributions are fully tax-deductible.